What people are saying about

The Energetic Dimension

Having known of Ann Drake͏ ʌad always been impressed with she had her shamanic training with a true ͏. ͏ysian Borneo and I was convinced that there we might find tɪɪᴄ source of her therapeutic success as a healer-psychotherapist. This books gives us insights into the underlying patterns that propelled her. Understandings emerging far outside the reaches of Western culture became an amalgam that makes her personal journey accessible to us all. It gives us pause to reflect upon the limits of the models with which we grew up that hold sway over our troubled Occidental culture. It provides a legitimate view from outside of the world within. A profound combination of Western and non-Western theory transforms the healing process. Ann Drake offers many paths, many destinations, with a single goal. Here is the secret of her success as a practitioner of the ancient art of healing.
Robert Bosnak, PsyA, founder, Santa Barbara Healing Sanctuary; author of *A Little Course in Dreams* and *Embodiment: Creative Imagination in Medicine, Art and Travel*

Ann Drake sees pain with eyes of wisdom and compassion, prompting us to look into our family myths and see beyond cultural biases in order to liberate our inherent creative and loving capacities as humans. She points to a necessary evolutionary step toward embracing both intellect and intuition on the healing journey.
Marcy Vaughn, internationally known senior student of Tenzin Wangyal Rinpoche

Ann Drake is a gifted and marvellous shamanic practitioner and teacher. In *The Energetic Dimension* she gifts us with a wealth of wisdom as to how our karma from previous incarnations and the relationships with our ancestors impacts our health and well-being on all levels. Ann shares with us her protocols and case studies for working with ancient practices that she has brilliantly adapted to heal the traumas of our times. I was so inspired by the work Ann shared in this timely book. *The Energetic Dimension* has critical work we all need to focus on to regain a state of balance in our lives. This is a must read!

Sandra Ingerman, award winning author of *Soul Retrieval* and The *Book of Ceremony: Shamanic Wisdom for Invoking the Sacred Into Everyday Life*

The Energetic Dimension

Understanding Our Karmic, Ancestral and Cultural Imprints

The Energetic Dimension

Understanding Our Karmic, Ancestral
and Cultural Imprints

Ann M. Drake, PsyD

BOOKS
Winchester, UK
Washington, USA

JOHN HUNT PUBLISHING

First published by O-Books, 2019
O-Books is an imprint of John Hunt Publishing Ltd., 3 East St., Alresford,
Hampshire SO24 9EE, UK
office@jhpbooks.com
www.johnhuntpublishing.com
www.o-books.com

For distributor details and how to order please visit the 'Ordering' section on our website.

ISBN: 978 1 78904 137 8
978 1 78904 138 5 (ebook)
Library of Congress Control Number: 2018945647

A CIP catalogue record for this book is available from the British Library.

Design: Stuart Davies

UK: Printed and bound by CPI Group (UK) Ltd, Croydon, CR0 4YY
US: Printed and bound by Thomson-Shore, 7300 West Joy Road, Dexter, MI 48130

We operate a distinctive and ethical publishing philosophy in all areas of our business, from our global network of authors to production and worldwide distribution.

Contents

To Josh, Tanya and Skylar who bring joy to my heart, and light and love to my world. And to all of you who have opened your hearts and souls to me and from whom I have learned so much. You have been my true teachers.

Acknowledgements

I first want to thank the amazing teachers that have graced my life. Ismail Daim, also known as the Bomoh, accepted me as an apprentice and generously shared with me the ancient wisdom from his indigenous healing practices of the jungles of Borneo and the Unani tradition that have transformed my life, brought healing to many and expanded my perception of reality. Tenzin Wangyal Rinpoche, Marcy Vaughn and Gabriel Rocco brought the rich teachings of the Bön Buddhists into my heart and soul providing a daily practice that brings both joy and peace to my life and is the foundation for the work that I do. The first time that I met Robert Bosnak, a renowned Jungian analyst, he asked me a simple question, "Where does your mother's energy live within you?" which awakened me to the reality of the energetic dimension of one's being.

Ellen Szabo, a gifted writer and teacher, brought form and structure to this book and urged me to paint pictures with words to convey the heart of the message. Patty Gift generously offered her time and considerable skill in guiding me through the process of creating a book proposal and of the importance of creating a social media platform. Roz Cummins tirelessly edited the book and with great humor attempted to teach me the ins and out of social media, a skill that I have yet to master. Her patience, warmth and encouragement has been a true gift and much appreciated. Michael Cooper, the publisher of my first book and a dear friend, served as a guide, critic and editor, alerting me to those moments when I became a bit too preachy or far out there. I want to thank all of the folks at O-Books for believing in my work and for bringing it to life and into the world. I want to thank my dear brothers and sisters of the Three Doors community for their ongoing love and support with a special shout out to my tarp sisters.

Most importantly I want to offer profound gratitude for all of my spirit guides and power animals who used me as the vehicle to bring their teachings into the world. I did not write this book; they wrote it through me.

Chapter 1

Introduction

In the early 1990s, I experienced a strong pull to return to the state of Sarawak in Malaysian Borneo where I had been a Peace Corps volunteer in the late 60s. I had lived and worked for over two years in a village named Matu that was three days by boat from the nearest town. It was a peaceful idyllic village that had no awareness of the existence of the United States and believed all white people came from New Zealand. I was the first white woman they had seen. There was no running water or electricity. Everyone bathed and drank from the same water in which they relieved themselves. As a result, there was an infant mortality rate of 50%. Needless to say, it took my body some time to adjust to these conditions as well. Often, I turned to the local shamans for healing as there was no other form of health care available. Once I was quite ill with a fever of 104. The local dukun, the name given to a female shaman, massaged my tense muscles, and when she was finished, my fever was gone. I marveled at her skill, never dreaming that years later, I would perform a healing for her after she had a stroke. I had no idea at the time how she was able to heal my ravaged body, but I did know that she had magic in her hands that I had never experienced before.

Muslims arrived on the coast of Northern Borneo in the 16th century and converted the people there to Islam. Despite this fact, when I was first arrived the women were bare breasted; today they are covered from head to toe in traditional Islamic dress. I knew little about Islam when I first lived in Matu and struggled to discern which of their healing practices and traditions came from the Islamic faith and which were indigenous to Borneo. A strong belief in spirit guides, ghosts, and elemental guides was pervasive. The air was filled with magic. The energy in Borneo

3

was markedly different from the United States, as if life existed on a different frequency or vibration. I was quite happy living there and felt a peace and connection to nature that I had not experienced in America. I had frequent *déjà vu* experiences while living in Matu opening me to consider the existence of past lives.

Before going into the Peace Corps, I had been quite interested in politics and the public arena, majoring in political science in college and minoring in history. In my time in Borneo I felt a pull to go inward. Upon my return, I was drawn to explore the psychological and spiritual aspects of existence. My husband was at Harvard Divinity School. I carried a secret longing that I could go there as well. Instead, I went to graduate school to become a school psychologist and then to start a family. After a twelve-year hiatus, I returned to graduate school to earn a doctorate in clinical psychology.

At the time of my return visit, I was working as a clinical psychologist in private practice and taught in a doctoral program in clinical psychology. My specialty was working with people who had experienced severe emotional, physical and sexual trauma, including those with dissociative identity disorder (DID), also known as multiple personality disorder. Often, I pondered how it was that one personality could inhabit a body and then seconds later a totally different being was before me. Frequently the various personalities had dissimilar physiology with one personality wearing glasses and the other with perfect sight. In another instance one personality had a severe case of asthma whereas the others were free of all asthmatic symptoms. Where did one personality or alter go when the other appeared, and how was it that the physical body was so different from one alter to the next? I could always tell in an instant which alter was with me as each looked, sounded and acted differently. A different energy about each one was apparent, as if an entirely different vibration ran through the body.

In the West, we are skilled at giving definition to what we

observe but less apt at truly understanding the phenomena before us. I asked colleagues how they conceptualized the process that allows different personalities to share the same body. I received rather dismissive responses such as, "your client switched" or "another alter emerged". These responses told me what anyone could have witnessed, but they did not tell me how this happens. Once I taught a seminar to medical students on dissociative identity disorder during which I described to them the phenomena of different and opposing physical symptoms within the same body. The medical students were unanimous in their opinion that it was not possible to have different physical symptoms within the same body; therefore, this proved that DID was the product of therapists' overactive imaginations. It seemed that if a given phenomenon could not be explained by one's existing paradigm, then it did not exist. I had hoped that the scientist within each of them would find such assertions mind expanding, but that was not the case. Instead, I was left to hope that on my long-awaited trip to Asia I might be exposed to another way of thinking that would help to solve this conundrum. Little did I know what lay in store for me!

My dear college friend Georgette and I planned a five-week trip through India, Nepal, Malaysian Borneo, Indonesia and Hong Kong. Georgette, a Jungian analyst, and I settled on a theme for the trip. We set out to discern how each culture understands the psychological and spiritual aspects of life. Since we were both academics, we hoped a paper or article might emerge from our inquiries. After all, our type A personalities would not permit us to wander through Asia without a purpose or focus. Georgette was particularly interested in talking with indigenous shamans. Many believe that Jung was himself a shaman, and Georgette was interested in learning more about this practice. At the time, I had not fully made the link that the wonderful healers I had encountered while in the Peace Corps were indeed shamans. I carried a stereotypical notion that shamans were bizarre, exotic, and a bit scary, and not the kind, caring people who were my friends and neighbors that also functioned as healers.

During our visit to Matu, Ismail Daim, the local shaman, invited my friend Georgette and I to travel with him to a distant village built entirely over water. We had been gathering at his house each evening. The Bomoh, which is the name given to male shamans, was the father of Yakuup, one of my former students, who as a government official spoke fairly comprehensible English. After a 22-year absence, my retention of the unwritten language of the people there had faded. Yakuup served as an excellent translator. In the distant village of Tian, there was a man who was dying. No one knew what was wrong with him so they sent for the Bomoh, as he was considered the best healer in the area. We arrived by boat, then climbed a rickety ladder into a house that was built on stilts over the water. The house was made of uneven wooden boards with a thatched roof of dried grass. There was no furniture. Everyone sat on the floor on hand-woven mats. The man was bloated and distended with a green pallor. He looked to be in his 80s although he was just 39. No one knew what was wrong with him. I took one look at him and thought that he might die at any moment. The Bomoh performed an elaborate ceremony. First, he prepared a green paste that he smeared over the man's body. He then covered him with newspaper, then waved knives above him while saying prayers and incantations. After the ceremony, the man began to stir. By evening he was sitting up and was able to eat. I asked the Bomoh what had been wrong with him and he told me that the man was a fisherman; his boat had capsized in the shark-infested waters of the South China Sea. In most instances, one would be eaten by a shark in a matter of moments. Fearing this, the man left his body anticipating his death, but he was rescued before he was attacked. The fear of being eaten alive was so strong that the fear and terror filled his energy body thereby making it impossible for the man's soul to return. Thus, his body was dying without the major part of his soul essence inhabiting it. The Bomoh later told me that all illness—whether physical, emotional or spiritual—is caused by two things: the loss of part of one's core essence, and the intrusion of other energies. In this case the fear and terror of being eaten alive by a shark had almost completely filled his energy body, leaving just a faint trace of his soul behind.

The Bomoh removed the traumatic energy from this terrifying event and the fear that enveloped him. Then he journeyed into non-ordinary reality to find the man's soul essence and brought it back to him. With his soul returned, he was able to return to full health. Chills spread throughout my body as I realized that at last I had answers to my questions. When one encounters a terrifying and traumatic event, one dissociates. Most have heard reports from people that were in a horrible car crash describe how they looked down on their bodies, unsure if they were alive or dead. In the moment of shock and horror when one is traumatized, one leaves the body. In this vacuum, one takes in the frightening energy of the horrifying event. As a result, one can stay traumatized for years after a life-threatening event as the energy of the trauma lives within the energy body of the person. This is why the vast majority of those who have served in war zones continue to experience the horrors of war decades after they have returned home. Fortunately, there are shamanic techniques to remove this energy and to bring back the parts of the soul essence that were lost, such as the Bomoh did.

As I pondered this new understanding, I expanded this awareness to those who had experienced emotional, physical or sexual abuse. I came to realize that one not only takes in the terrifying energy of that event, but also aspects of the person that is harming them. The violent negative energy flows into the vacuum where part of the soul essence once had been. This explained why every person that I worked with that had dissociative identity disorder had another personality or alter that was just like the person that harmed them. The energy, voice and a part of the essence of the abuser lived within, incessantly tormenting their victim, often driving them mad or causing them to appear to be psychotic. Sometimes this perpetrating alter reenacts the core trauma through self-abuse or the actual abuse of another in the same manner in which the person originally was abused. This is a very important concept to grasp as it can alter how we understand PTSD and the so-called "acting out" or "destructive" behavior of survivors of trauma. It is my hope as well that we can begin to develop compassion and understanding for those who are perpetrators, as the vast majority of perpetrators were abused in the same manner that they are harming others. Through shamanic extraction and soul retrieval, these damaging energies can be healed and transformed and the part of the soul or essence that left through the process of being traumatized can be healed and brought back, thereby returning the soul to wholeness.

The day before Georgette and I were to leave Matu, the Bomoh informed us that his guides instructed him to initiate us to the path of the shaman. At first I did not know what to think as I had no idea what this really meant or precisely what a shaman did. Even though I received remarkable healings on more than one occasion, by what I now understand were local shamans when I was in the Peace Corps, I did not fully comprehend what they did or how they did it. I must also confess that in the late 60s, I carried the bias that Western health care was far superior to indigenous healers, rather than an understanding that both have value. Little did I know that my life would change in fundamental and wondrous ways if I accepted the call to this path. I did accept the initiation as a voice within was clear that I was to do this. When I returned to the US, I found that the study and practice of shamanism were alive and vibrant throughout the entire country, and that there were many wonderful teachers with whom to take workshops and study. The Bomoh had initiated me into the Unani tradition of shamanism through a series of transmissions, which contained a rich system of guides and protectors for my energetic body. As a result of this, I was energetically deeply embedded within this tradition. Given that my teacher was half a world away with a 13-hour time difference, crackly phone lines and language challenges, I was basically on my own. Weekly I asked the guides what I was to study and learn to deepen my knowledge of this path. They directed me to learn about the energy body, the chakra system, and the dreambody.

Since it was before the era where one could push the search button or ask one's smartphone a question, I went to the local "New Age" bookstore and found to my amazement that there was a plethora of books, from various countries and a variety of perspectives, written about our energy system. How could we in the West be so ignorant of this way of understanding how humans function, when the non-Western world has understood and worked with this knowledge for thousands of years? I consumed this new knowledge like a person starving to understand something, which on one level I knew, but on another was just outside of my grasp. It is fascinating that just as the people in Matu had no knowledge of the United States in the late sixties, we had no knowledge of the wisdom that these other cultures held. There is a bias in the West that our paradigm of health and healing is far superior to "less developed countries", when in fact, we leave out the energetic basis of our existence. The dualistic paradigm of only scientifically considering as real what is concretely observed has blinded us to the energetic aspect of our being and of existence itself. Through quantum physics and string theory there is the acknowledgement that there are multiple levels of reality and different vibrational frequencies. Centuries ago the Hindus came to understand that we all have a dreambody that is the vehicle in which we travel as our soul essence comes into a physical body when we are born and is the vehicle from which we exit the body at the time the body dies.

Within the dreambody is every vibration of every experience that we have had throughout each lifetime. We are energetic and vibrational beings.

As I deepened my shamanic practice and study, I became aware that there were aspects of shamanism in each of the major theoretical schools of psychology and that each of these schools could be further illuminated by an understanding of the energy body and how it works. This inspired me to write a book entitled, *Healing of the Soul: Shamanism and Psyche*. From a shamanic perspective, there is energy in everything. There are many levels of healing the soul, the psyche, and the physical body, which range from the micro or inner world of a person, to the macro or societal context. Everything from a cut on the hand to occurrences that happen in the larger world go into the health and well-being of a person and of the planet. As I noted before, the Bomoh told me that there are two reasons for all illness, be it physical, spiritual or emotional: the loss of part of the core essence of a person, and the intrusion of other energies to fill the void left by this soul loss. We easily understand how the intrusion of germs or disease fills our body and makes us sick, but we are less likely to consciously grasp the extent to which hateful words and the negative energy behind these words can pierce the heart and wound the soul. We can see and experience the damage done to individuals and communities by a powerful storm but are less likely to readily assess the damage done to the health and well-being of citizens by living with a constant stream of fear and hate flowing through the airways.

Psychological theories such as psychodynamic and object relation theories deal with the inner or intrapsychic life of a person. These theories come very close to understanding the energetic exchange between people. They talk of introjects, which is the taking in of part of another into the deep recess of the psyche, and conversely projections in which one places unprocessed aspects of our own psyche onto another. Novels and films are ripe with images of the wounded father who feels grossly inadequate and spews this inadequacy onto his sons by calling them stupid and worthless as he beats them senseless. These self-hating projections are taken in by the sons who painfully carry the mantle of self-loathing. The energy of the hate is absorbed into the energetic body and is anchored by the cognitive structures of the mind. The words, "You are stupid and worthless," become beliefs or thought forms that the child assumes to be true. This energy and the accompanying beliefs form the foundation of the ancestral imprints. Often the message of worthlessness and self-loathing is passed from generation to generation. Cognitive behavioral therapy teaches people how to ignore or manage these unwanted negative beliefs. As a result of the energetic base of these thoughts, it is hard to let them go. If it were easy, we would all blithely ignore the notion that we are stupid the first time we got an A on a test proving that we are not. One can be a straight A student and still feel stupid or like a fraud when the person who knows them best repeatedly proclaims they are stupid. Systemic theories take into account the role that family dynamics play in shaping who we are. In many families, there is a scapegoat; the person that holds all of the negative energy and beliefs for the family. Rarely is there a meeting to elect a person to carry this role, but through an unspoken energetic communication the person is subtly chosen. This theory views each person through a contextual lens that takes into account not only the family context, but also the community, cultural, spiritual beliefs and customs. In shamanism, everything is interconnected. Nothing stands alone.

We often come close to understanding the energetic base of our existence. Many of us already grasp it on the intuitive level but fail to fully take in the level to which we are energetically connected and the power of these energies to shape who we are and how we operate in the world. How many times have we heard someone exclaim that their mother/partner/sister sucks the life out of them or that they feel drained after being with them? In this book we will explore the depths to which our ancestral lineage shapes who we are for good or ill. We will delve into the karmic influences that are carried from one lifetime to another and shed new understanding on how siblings that grow up in the same family can be so radically different. The role that gender, class, race, religion, culture and nation/state play in influencing how we perceive reality cannot be underestimated. In addition, the generation and region of the country to which we are born shapes, in profound ways, who we are. A black girl coming of age in the South in the 1950s has a radically different way of experiencing the world than a white male growing up in California in the 1970s.

This book explores the energetic web in which we are encased, ways to cultivate its strengths, and heal and remove the negative aspects of unwanted energies. The goal is to be able to shed the layers that block us from truly experiencing our core essence and who we truly are. In shamanism, there are spirit guides and power animals that support, protect and teach us throughout our lives. They help enormously in discerning our true nature. Their role in many ways is analogous to the function that patron saints and other religious deities play in all of the major religions of the world. Some of the concepts may be challenging to grasp at first glance. There is a glossary of terms to consult at the end of the book.

Part I

A Path to Wholeness

Chapter 2

Power of the Energetic

One of the goals of this book is to foster the paradigm shift that allows us to first fathom and then work with energy to manifest the world that we want, both personally and collectively. We understand the energetic base of our existence on an intuitive level, but there are those that do not yet grasp the power that we have to shift these vibrations, both personally, within our communities, and throughout the world. Through shamanic and energy work, it is possible to heal and transform energies that we have absorbed from others, that have been left behind when our energy was taken or are the energetic vibration of traumatic events. These healing techniques also have the power to heal traumatic events that we carried from one lifetime to the next. How the energetic impacts the physical will be explored in depth as the book unfolds.

Energy

We are energy. All matter, including our physical bodies, are merely slowed down energy. Each of us has an energetic field that extends from the physical body out to the tips of our fingers on outstretched arms that swirls holographically within and around our physical body. We also have a dreambody that attaches at the solar plexus, slightly above our midline, and to the kidneys in the back. Within the dreambody the vibrations of every experience and memory from our present throughout all of our previous lifetimes dance in and out of consciousness as they are triggered by our daily experiences. Housed within the dreambody is our soul essence, which enters the body at birth and leaves at the death of the body.[1]

An awareness of the energetic base of our existence goes back at least 60,000 years when the practice of shamanism was believed to be present throughout the world. For eons humans were cognizant not only of the energetic connection among one another, but also of their connection with all that is. Before the modern era, the natural environment and all the creatures within vibrated with energy that was perceived and respected by human beings. The natural environment is still vibrating with energy, but most humans have lost the ability to see and experience this.

The interdependence among beings: the humans, the four legged, the winged ones, the elements, plants, trees and rocks was intuitively part of consciousness.

Today we turn on the TV or check the Internet to learn what is happening in the world. In the past one engaged all senses to discern what was occurring around us. No weather report or fancy machine was needed to predict an upcoming storm. One could read the energy of the air and sky while observing the behavior of the critters in the area. Before the tsunami struck Phuket in '04, the elephants broke free of their chains scrambling uphill into the rain forest to escape the monstrous waves. Many lives might have been saved if the humans had followed their lead.

Instead of shared instinct, many today turn to electronic gadgets dismissing and dulling the intuitive awareness of the energetic web around and within. Through the media we are told what to think and what is trending while ceasing to listen to the wisdom within and around us. The dulling of our senses renders us fertile ground for manipulation. By denying the energetic dimension of our being and the energetic connection between us and our environment we surrender a key resource of information. Instead of honoring a sense of foreboding in entering a given situation, more often than not we reject it as silliness, sadly to our own peril. When I trace back to every major mistake that I made in my life, I can see that I ignored the intuitive and energetic information that I *knew* to be true. Conversely, when I listened to this inner wisdom, all flowed effortlessly as exemplified by the pull to return to Borneo in the early nineties without knowing why.

Our energetic interconnectedness is similar to the workings of social media and the World Wide Web. Energetically we are impacted by each person that we come into contact with, and this energy expands in all directions like the wind wafting through and around us. Notice, when walking into a large conference or party, how within moments we have an intuitive sense of whom we want to approach and whom we want to avoid. How do we know this? There are energetic vibrations that spread out connecting us to others. Some might feel familiar, as if they are known to us. Others might feel dangerous; perhaps they energetically feel like someone who has harmed us in some way. There might be a past life connection that draws us to someone like a magnet; whereas another might repel us. These quick assessments arise without uttering a word or gathering any "concrete" information. Often, unaware, we read the energy around us and around those we encounter. We watch a celebrity or politician on TV and form a sense of them almost instantly. We establish social, community and political affiliations based on beliefs but also on how we energetically resonate with the people involved. Occasionally I meet someone that I do not agree with spiritually or politically but find myself genuinely liking them for who they are and the sense of comfort that I feel in their presence. There is an energetic resonance that overrides rational thought. To understand better how all of this works, let us begin with the energetics of the individual to discover how each of us impacts and is impacted by the energy of others, our culture and nation state.

Soul Loss

As stated earlier, my shamanic teacher purported that all illness, be it physical, emotional or spiritual, is caused by two things: the loss of part of our core essence energy and the intrusion of other energies. These energies can be anything from germs and bacteria that can attack the physical body to negative emotional states or traumatic events that fill the body with the energies of fear, hate and violence while part of the core essence pops out. It is not uncommon to hear someone say, "He was never the same after his surgery." During surgery it is extremely common for parts of the soul to leave the body while it is being cut open. Post-surgery, though the body may return to full health, a part of the soul or core essence might remain hiding in a corner of the operating room. If there is frantic energy flying around during the surgery, this energy may enter the energetic body of the patient, leaving a high state of anxiety where part of the core essence was. When energy leaves the body, it leaves a space for other energy to come in. As long as this anxiety is filling the energetic body, it is challenging for the soul part to reenter. These energetic exchanges can be as damaging to the soul as MRSA is to the body. There are myriad opportunities to pick up energies from others each day—from schools, churches, hospitals, grocery stores and most significantly from family and friends. If we have not experienced soul loss, although it is rare that one has not, then it is hard for these energies to come fully into our energetic body. Again, this can be healed via shamanic extraction and soul retrieval.

Ancestral and Karmic Imprints

The energetic imprint of the family is absorbed into our field in infancy and most likely in utero. Like our telecommunication system we are comprised of energy waves. If we are born into a family that has a depressed energy, a sense of not being good enough, or a sense of self-hate and self-deprecation, we may absorb these energetic waves and they become part of our energetic body. Conversely, if we are born into a family that is confident and believes that anything is possible, we absorb this energy as well. We perceive these energetic states as who we are, when in reality these energetic states may obscure our true nature, who we truly are. The ancestral imprint to which we are born not only has a cognitive base that teaches us a particular way of viewing reality, but also an energetic base that influences how we experience reality.

As a psychologist, I have sat session after session with clients who could not see their beauty and worth even though there was ample external validation for this. No rational reviewing of their strengths can counter the energetic imprint of worthlessness until this dimension is fully understood by them. The sense of worthlessness may stem from being told from an early age that one will not amount to anything, but it may also be absorbed from being treated in a manner that implies that they are of no value; an assertion of being worthless is not needed as it is so strongly felt. The sense of worthlessness may also arise from an ancestral imprint that is felt and passed from one generation to the next as clearly as curly hair or brown eyes are inherited.

These energetic waves then interact with others of similar energetic vibrations. If a child is repeatedly berated and beaten with scant opportunity to heal this pattern, then, most likely, that child will grow up to partner with someone of a similar energetic vibration. How many times does a woman go from one abusive partner to the next? Society often chides her for her stupidity in doing the same thing again and again. As a result of the lack of awareness of the energetic waves that draw her to what is known, to what reverberates on a core energetic level and to what she feels she deserves as a result of these negative imprints and treatment, she continues to be drawn to the same painful relationships feeling even more self-disparaging. In turn, her children will likely absorb this same imprint and the cycle of abuse will repeat itself. Fortunately, there are ways to heal and transform these energetic states that will be explored in depth as the book unfolds. The depths to which our ancestral lineage shapes who we are for good or ill is examined. The book delves into the karmic influences that are carried from one lifetime to another and sheds new understanding on how siblings that grow up in the same family can be so radically different.

Not surprisingly, an emerging global consciousness has awakened the vibrational imprints of our previous incarnations, which brings new energies into the core aspect of our personal energy field and new dimensions to the energetic web that inhabits our energy fields. This in turn expands and interacts with the collective expanded fields all around us. We feel drawn to explore places or take up causes in parts of the world that were scarcely in our consciousness a few decades ago. These karmic imprints stir faint memories of both positive and negative incarnations, and unconsciously inform our opinions in subtle ways. One of the greatest gifts in my life was the opportunity to live in this lifetime in a village that was essentially unchanged from when I had lived there in a previous incarnation, to re-experience firsthand the peace and joy as well as the considerable hardship of living totally connected to nature, to community and to the sense of oneness with all that is.

Our karmic lineages carry the many lessons we have gathered from one lifetime to the next. But they also carry the wounds, misconceptions and cultural baggage from these incarnations. We wear the energies of these experiences like an old weathered coat. Added to these energies are the imprints of our ancestral lineage. Some of these imprints may be great gifts that manifest as traits such as courage, strength, and compassion, but we may also carry the burden of fear, shame, and disconnection. Shadow remnants of hate and rage that birth the tendency towards war, greed, racism and a sense of entitlement which put our needs and pleasures above our neighbors and all of the creatures and beings on the planet keep us from our true hearts. When the tendencies that encourage war and greed are heralded as the cornerstone of a culture, our true nature can be eclipsed altogether. Perhaps our true nature is not to be violent, wrathful and greedy, perhaps these are the energies that we have absorbed from the past and can be shed, healed and transformed. Lifetimes in which we lived in peace and harmony lie within as well, and may stir within us a longing to return to the sense of a loving connected lifetime.

The World Wide Web and Energy

Throughout the world, many cultures have an understanding of the energetic basis of our existence. Disruption in the flow of energy renders the body out of balance and results in illness. For centuries acupuncture and Qigong have been the cornerstone of the Chinese health care system, which is energetically based. In these systems, there are meridians that flow throughout the body. If there is an energetic block in these meridians, then illness may ensue. Through energy work and acupuncture the meridians are cleared so that the system flows naturally. Fascinated I watched a video of a healing performed by Qigong energy workers in a Qigong hospital in China. They stood around the bed of a person with a tumor who was connected to a CAT scanner. Riveted I observed the tumor shrink until it dissolved as these amazing healers stood stationary, hands outstretched over the tumor in the body. I marveled at the positive results that were obtained in a mere twenty minutes without the intrusion of surgery, chemo or radiation.

In addition to acupuncture and Qigong, the chakra system an ancient metaphysical system originated in India. There are seven major chakras, forty secondary chakras and 88,000 minor ones, leaving scarcely a dot on our bodies that is not open for the reception, transmission or transformation of energy.[2] There are many practitioners that balance and clear the chakras through energy work, shamanic work, sound healing, flower essences, and work with crystals. A shadow industry of traditional healers has emerged and is steadily growing. Many consumers realize the limitations of allopathic medicine due to its lack of awareness of the energetic basis of our being. Many, when confronted with a life-threatening or chronic illness, either turn exclusively to an energetic system of healing or use it to complement Western medicine. Some extend the awareness of the energetic base of our being to the psychological and emotional arena. In my experience, rarely is talk therapy enough to heal emotional difficulties. Through the introduction of shamanic and energetic techniques for the treatment of mental illness and emotional problems, the psyche is healed to a greater extent and within a much shorter time frame. When I performed a soul retrieval for a client who suffered from sexual trauma and depression, I removed the energy of the trauma from her field and brought back soul parts that had been healed from abuse and despair. The client soon felt remarkably improved, a sense of wholeness flowing throughout where depression had lived. A couple of months later, she joked that I should charge $4,000 for a soul retrieval as we had just lopped off two years of therapy.

Most cultures have a long-standing herbal tradition for health and healing. Within this is the awareness of the energetic vibration of the plant and how to enhance this vibration with spiritual energy. In the early 1990s the Bomoh found a tree bark in the heart of the rain forest that could heal HIV/AIDS. His skill in healing with this bark was well known within Sarawak. The Bomoh frequently was asked to come into Western hospitals to heal those with HIV/AIDS. He was given a white doctor's coat to wear by the Malaysian government. A Western pharmaceutical company learned of his great skill with the tree bark and promptly offered him more money than he could ever imagine amassing in a lifetime to show them the tree from which he found the bark. Honorably he refused, saying that without the interaction of spiritual energy with the plant it would not be effective. He gave me some of this bark and taught me how to use it for remarkable results. Over time the pharmaceutical industry discovered the tree and learned how to make a synthetic version that sadly is often tainted with the energy of greed, rather than the healing energy of the spiritually infused bark. Herbalists often purport that all we need to heal is growing right in our own communities. Given the high cost of pharmaceuticals, many are turning to herbal and homeopathic remedies to strengthen the immune system and heal various maladies. Through the emergence of a global consciousness and the availability of knowledge through the World Wide Web, incredible ancient healing methods are brought to light.

Vibrations, Power Animals and Spirit Guides

In shamanism there are spirit guides and power animals that support, protect and teach us throughout our lives. They help enormously in discerning our true nature. Their role in many ways is analogous to the function that patron saints and other religious deities play in all of the major religions of the world. I consulted with a trusted mentor and channel when I first began treating clients who had cancer. I had concerns that as I extracted the cancerous imprint in the tumors from the body I might be at risk of bringing the vibration of cancer into my own body. She paused reflectively for a moment and then replied that cancer exists on every vibration, and in order for me to work with clients that have cancer, I need to make sure that my energetic body is protected on each vibrational level. Then she told me that I was missing the vibration of eel urging me to cultivate a relationship with eel.

This revelation was quite enlightening and also stimulated several questions for me to discuss with my spirit guides and power animals. Each of us has a core guide that has been with us since birth. In the West, we are not raised to know or honor this connection; whereas in many other cultures it is an awareness that is passed from parent to child and is widely acknowledged within the culture. In the Native American tradition, one has a major power animal that is both teacher and protector throughout one's life. It is also possible for a healer to find and bring to a client a power animal or spirit guide that embodies the vibration that the client most needs at this time. If a client is in need of strength and confidence, one might ask for a lion, bear or buffalo; if one needs love and compassion, a spirit guide that holds this vibration may be called upon. Whenever I perform a healing for another in which I bring back a soul part that has been hurt or traumatized, I also bring back a spirit guide or power animal for this healed part to assist with integration of this part back into the core essence of the client.

In Borneo I received several different spirit and elemental guides through a ritual of transmission. Transmissions of teachings, power animals, spirit guides and deities are common in many of the spiritual traditions in the East. Sometimes the process of transmission is quite simple, sometimes quite complex and elaborate. Some teachers chant sacred text, using bells and singing bowls to carry the vibration of the transmissions into the field of their students. More dramatically the Bomoh placed the energy to be transmitted into a bucket of water, then pointed the tip of a knife into my crown chakra while simultaneously chanting prayers and pouring the bucket of water into my crown, drenching me in the sacred water. In one of my visits to my teacher, the Bomoh blessed me with the transmission of a powerful seven-headed sea genii that is comprised of hurricane energy that is both water and wind. It has been invaluable in sucking out unwanted energy that is stuck in the body of my clients. A year later I received a crocodile spirit in a ritual in which, unknown to me at the time, I was swimming in a river with crocodiles. He informed me after the second transmission that I could not use these two powerful guides simultaneously until my energy body was strong enough to hold and work with both of these energetic vibrations concurrently. As one might lift weights to strengthen the body, I needed to strengthen my energetic body through the healing work that I did and daily rituals of integration of these very powerful guides until such time that my energetic body was able to comfortably manage these very powerful energetic vibrations simultaneously.

It is important to comprehend that power animals, spiritual guides and elemental energies are vibrations. I do not literally have a crocodile living with me, but the base vibration of the crocodile that has lived on the planet since the time of the dinosaurs is part of my energetic field. In Sarawak, there are crocodile farms, as crocodiles are considered sacred, but are also known to attack and eat humans. As a result of the need to both honor these magnificent beings and protect the people, crocodiles are brought to a farm that is enclosed within fences over hundreds of acres of land. Humans stroll the farm encased in caged walkways. I rather like the idea of putting people in the cages while allowing the crocodiles to roam free. I visited this farm in Sarawak in order to discern the nature of the crocodile. I stayed the entire day, standing still as I stared intently at these powerful creatures. After five to ten minutes of locked gazes, I silently spoke to the crocodile with whom I was communing, "If you can see my crocodile spirit, please open your mouth." Within seconds of communicating this sentiment, the crocodile opened his mouth. I performed the same ritual with three different crocodiles. Each crocodile opened his mouth wide upon my request. They were able to perceive the vibration of the crocodile within my energy body, and through this vibration, I was able to communicate with them.

It may seem fanciful that one can communicate with animals in this manner, but this is a skill that many of our wise ancestors had and that many still have to date. Today they are called animal communicators. These wise communicators are able to shift their vibration in order to connect to the vibration of the animal with which they are communing. To our ancestors, it would seem just as farfetched to communicate by texting with our phones. As we settle into the awareness that everything has a vibrational energy that we can tune into with our heart and mind, we begin to fathom that we are all part of the same whole. Rocks hold a vibration that is ancient and wise, trees have a strength and gentleness that grounds us to the physical plane. Humans are merely part of the vibrational makeup of the planet earth. The earth has its own vibration that distinguishes it from other planets and we are part of this vibration.

A Time of Transformation

We are entering a period of profound transformation on the planet. Daily we are confronted with the awareness of our interconnectedness. Economic markets throughout the world rise and fall in unison. From the US and China toxic fumes float into the air space of their neighbors choking them with plumes of unbreathable pollution. The World Wide Web connects people from every corner of the world. Mass movements come into being with the click of a mouse. The blending of races and cultures has produced a new generation in which historically important distinctions are no longer relevant. Gradually we take in the notion that we are all one, that our survival and happiness are intricately linked with one another.

For the past three decades, our planet's astrological alinements have facilitated and urged us to open our hearts and minds to a much larger sense of our interconnectedness. Yet many continue to damage the planet and our souls by furthering a path of violence, war, greed and the perverse need to view ourselves as superior not only to other groups of people, but also to all of the creatures and elemental energies on the planet. The vibration of violence harms us energetically. Throughout my lifetime, I have pondered why we are so mean to one another. Often, I have been told that this is the nature of man. Through these current astrological alignments, we have the opportunity to shift vibrational patterns and thought forms such as the defensive belief of harming another before they harm us. We have the capacity to shed and heal the vibrations of fear, violence and greed that are at the root of so many problems.

What happens on the personal or micro level affects the

societal or macro realm. Through understanding how we contribute to negative vibrations on a personal level, we more readily grasp how everything is influenced energetically. When we have a fight with a friend, family member or lover, we are often deeply impacted by this. Frequently we cannot sleep or eat well; we spend hours in our mind going over the conflict. Sometimes we assure ourselves of the rightness of our position and grow the anger to proportions that far exceed the original misunderstanding. If the rupture is deep, we become obsessed with the conflict, thinking of it all the time and getting anyone we can corner to listen to our lament. Consumed energetically by the conflict, the obsessional energy flows from us to the estranged person, intensifying the energetic bond, albeit with negativity. Our agitation may also spread to those around us, sprinkling them with ions of pain and suffering. War, violence and greed have a similar way of fanning out, impacting us all on the macro level.

Cultural Imprints and the Collective Energetic Field

Personal pain flowing into the collective energetic field is exemplified through problems with the insurance industry and health care system. How we view the issue of health care often is influenced by cultural imprints such as our age, economic status and political party, and significantly whether we receive health care through our employment or do not. Ancestral and karmic imprints may also affect our point of view. For several decades there has been a growing angst over the cost of premiums, high deductibles, and until the Affordable Care Act, the denial of coverage for preexisting conditions. A single major illness had the power to wipe out a family's life savings, throwing them into bankruptcy, adding more stress to an already challenged family system. As more and more households faced economic catastrophe from a major illness, an energetic groundswell emerged that called out for relief. President Obama won his first term in office, in part, over his pledge to reform health care. Some of the goals of the Affordable Care Act were to provide health care for all, do away with preexisting conditions, and to return emergency rooms to emergencies rather than a clinic for the non-insured. His plan had been to have both public and private options for health care. The powerful insurance industry had other ideas and were able to influence enough legislatures to block a much cheaper and more effective public option similar to Medicare thereby placing the insurance industry in full charge of health care for all but those who qualify for Medicare and Medicaid type programs.

The influences of our cultural imprints strongly impact how one views the Affordable Care Act. Many young healthy people had opted out of buying health insurance, throwing the dice that nothing would happen to them, having many more uses for their money than the high cost of health care. Many resented being forced to buy health care and even chose the penalty rather than acquiesce. Senior citizens, on the other hand, almost to a person, love their Medicare and will be in the streets if attempts are made to take it away or radically change it; this signifies how the cultural imprint of age strongly affects one's point of view.

People resent high deductibles and co-pays yet are loath to spend more for health insurance than for their mortgages. Frustrated by brief office visits that usually end in more tests and/or a referral to a specialist that might tend to a problem with the feet, but not the leg, dissatisfaction grows by leaps and bounds creating an energetic movement. Many spend days going from one specialist to another with scant information as to what is wrong. Once the problem is diagnosed, the insurance company signs off on the treatment frequently overriding the best advice of the physician for a less costly option. Often one needs the IQ of a rocket scientist and the ability to read the incomprehensible language that only a lawyer can decipher to understand the various policies, plans and fine print only to find that the services one most needs are not covered. The collective frustration of the masses reached a boiling point and found a home in two diametrically opposed political positions.

Establishment politicians and political pundits were stunned into denial and disbelief at the rise of populist movements that spawned the Trump and Sanders candidacies in 2016. There was an energetic base to these movements that escaped the mindset and awareness of the establishment pols. Although Sanders and Trump are on the opposite side of the political divide, they each had the ability to *read* the dissatisfaction of the populous and to create a message that resonated with their followers. This is especially true regarding the frustrations surrounding health care. Those who believe that Obamacare is responsible for all of the health care woes flocked to the candidacy of Trump. He promised to abolish Obamacare without much thought as to what would replace it beyond a vague pledge that it would make America great again. For many that vague promise is enough to settle the layers of collective frustration. Those that believe that private insurance companies' control over health care should be abolished with a governmental single payer system clustered around Sanders trusting that health care costs will go down when the profit-hungry insurance companies are out of the mix. I believe that the collective energy of frustration regarding the health care system is one of the core reasons that these two radically diverse movements gained such traction. The individual frustration with the health care system grew to form a collective passionate movement, a movement on both the right and left that has an energetic base that often defies logic and rationality.

It can be argued that the lack of awareness in the energetic base of our existence limits the success of our health care system as allopathic medicine leaves out the foundation of our health and well-being, the energetic dimension. Frustrated, clients come to see me when they have been told by their medical doctors that they have no idea what is wrong with them and that "it must all be in their heads." Trauma and emotional upset have the power to alter the physical dimension of the body as is exemplified in my work with those with multiple personalities. If the energetic base of the trauma and emotional distress is healed, the physical body often returns to health and well-being.

One of the goals of this book is to expand our understanding of the many factors that shape our perception of reality and to discern what is truly reflective of our true essence rather than what we have absorbed from our ancestors, culture, and previous incarnations. Another goal is to develop a greater sense of compassion and equanimity for those with whom we disagree and do not understand. Many factors make each of us who we are; often we are trapped in energetic fields that do not reflect who we truly are. In addition, each of us wears blinders as a result of our imprints that prevent us from seeing each other as we truly are.

As the energy of the planet shifts into a lighter and more heart-centered vibration that honors and celebrates the beauty and grace in our interconnection with all that is, we need to unburden ourselves from the negative energies that we carry from our ancestral, karmic and cultural lineages. The fallout from these negative energies unraveling might feel as if they will bury us and any hope for peace. Yet as these energies leave our field, we will feel a lightness and joy that will carry us to a new consciousness.

When we sit in community with an open and compassionate heart, not only for oneself, but for others as well, then miraculous things may occur. It is in community that we find our heart and our healing. As we make the shift to a new planetary vibration, it is imperative to alter our stance from a sense of me and mine into the larger perspective that we are all part of the whole. When we work together powerful and magical things may happen. One by one as we shed the negative imprints from the past, these energies are released from the planet as we move closer to the world that we want to manifest.

Chapter 3

Reflections from the Red Garuda Retreat

It was two days after the shootings at Virginia Tech. I was on retreat with Tenzin Wangyal Rinpoche, a gifted and wise teacher of the Bön Buddhist tradition. Rinpoche established a sacred and peaceful retreat center in the hills of southern Virginia, called Serenity Ridge. The retreat was on, "The Healing Practices of the Red Garuda". It is an ancient practice designed to remove all obstacles and to burn off negative energies. The Garuda is my main spirit guide so I arrived at the retreat full of expectations. In the first few days, my mind wandered to inconsequential things. I experienced, in a more pronounced way than I had at other meditation retreats, the unruly nature of my mind that kept me focused on the mundane and away from the essence and energy of the teachings. The desire to break free from small mind was palpable as I struggled through the maze of gray energy that kept me bound. There were moments when I fell into the space that is oneness with all. The joy, energy, and power of this would fill my being, but within moments the small busy mind returned.

From Knowing to Experiencing

The experience that I had at the Red Garuda retreat opened the pathway for me to intuitively know and experience the power of the ancestral imprint that I had been encased within my entire life. The year prior to this retreat, the old patterns and imprints that I had naively believed were, at long last, healed and transformed were back staring me in the face. Long ago I forgave my mother for her over-controlling and abusive behavior—behaviors that undoubtedly stemmed from how controlled and stifled she felt as a woman of her generation. I felt compassion for how difficult it must have been to raise a spirited and fiercely independent daughter when she felt forced to live a life designed by others. It was easy to sustain love and compassion for her when I lived 1,000 miles away. During the illness and death of my father, I spent more time with my mother. My caring feelings were unwavering. Soon after my father's death, I moved my mother to a lovely assisted living facility near me. My parents had lived into their nineties; they had few friends still alive; most of the family had either died or moved away. I suggested that she come to live near me with no thought as to what might arise within me. I am certain that spirit orchestrated the move so that I would receive the teachings that I most dearly needed.

My mom bravely moved from the Midwest to the East Coast at the age of 93. She was in a new facility, and in many ways, a different culture. As the only family and familiar face in the area, I was her anchor. Initially her new surroundings excited her. I spent quite a bit of time with her as she became settled and oriented. My son was married a few months after she arrived. Excitement reigned with all of the wedding preparations in which she was happily involved. The entire extended family came to the wedding, and as the matriarch, my mother was in her glory. A month after the festivities were over, the mother that I had known and struggled with as a child began to emerge. The littlest thing upset her; the complaints about her situation were constant and unceasing. I tried with compassion to understand how hard it must be to have lost her husband of 65 years, then move from the only place that she had ever lived to a place where the people are more reserved and where she felt alone.

Despite my heartfelt understanding, I felt myself pulled back into the unspoken feeling state of my childhood, a state in which I felt powerless to make her happy without surrendering the basic essence of who I am. Often I felt protective and shut down around her. I was simultaneously resentful and guilty for not being able to anticipate what it was she needed. In my open heart, I knew that what she wanted was to hold on to as much of herself as she could while she drew me near so as not to face the end of her life alone. Although she did not state it, the child part of me believed that she wanted me to put my life on hold, to focus all of my time and energy on her, and to be the perfect daughter that she had intended me to be from the start—a daughter that anticipated her needs, lovingly sacrificed her own needs for the needs of her family, and was always cheerful and neatly dressed.

When I was a child, I was beaten and frozen out of her heart when I did not behave and *be* as she wanted me to be. Often, I had no idea what I had done wrong or what was considered a bad action. My mother frequently said that if I did not know what I had done, then she was not going to tell me. Credit is due her for the early development of my psychic abilities. As a small child, I fought back and struggled to steel myself from further hurt by her. There are stories that I held my breath until I would pass out if I did not get my way or that I would hold my body rigid until I could slip from her grasp and run from the house. At four, I changed my name and spent as much time as I could at the elderly neighbors across the street in a vain attempt to escape from the anger and abuse. In hindsight, it was clear that my defiant response only increased my mother's anger and frustration and yielded me the opposite of what I truly wanted— her love and acceptance.

In the sixties and seventies, I stood on the other side of the political divide from her as a political and cultural radical. My spiritual practices evolved over time to be considerably different in form from hers. As a devout Christian, she had difficulty understanding the core philosophy of Buddhism and shamanism, and worried that I had been taken over by a cult. My mother perceived my spiritual beliefs and practices as an affront to her and referred to them disparagingly as "Buddhuvoodu." I teetered on the edge of feeling both anger and sadness at being so unseen and unknown. Concurrently I felt compassion and love for her and her plight as an elderly widow.

As time wore on, I found myself second-guessing everything

that I did. I began to lose confidence in myself, a confidence that for the previous twenty years had been unshakable. Fortunately, due to the spiritual nature of my work and my deep connection to my guides, I was spared these recriminations in my professional life. Long ago I had given up the oppositional stance of my childhood. With the defiant defense that had protected me as a child gone, all of the early feelings were fully present. The ancestral imprint of shame and unworthiness had arisen from its resting place in my energy field to stare me straight in the face. Although for the most part, I understood and managed these feelings outwardly, inwardly I sunk deeper into confusion unable to shift the energy that enveloped me.

Oddly there were few angry words or condemnations from my mother; rather she often lavished praise and appreciation for all that I did for her, while simultaneously complaining about what others were not doing for her. I asked myself, "Where do these feelings come from? How are they being evoked?" It was then that I realized that I had fallen back into the affective state of my childhood. After deep meditation and journey work, I came to understand that the sheer proximity to my mother and her unmet needs had sucked me back into the energetic field of the family imprint. I experienced myself as re-engulfed by it and felt the terror that I had endured as a child when I felt frozen by the fear of annihilation of my basic essence or the loss of my primary attachment. In that childhood place I *felt* that I had to choose between loss of self or the loss of connection. Underlying this struggle was the sense that something was fundamentally wrong with me as I apparently was incapable of being who she wanted me to be. Although I understood what was happening, I found myself trapped in a daily struggle to propel myself out of this dreadful feeling state.

As I talked to my guides to understand what was happening, I was shown that I was back in the energy field of my ancestors. My parents were a puritanical blend of German, Scottish, and Welsh with the shame-based and obsessional energy of the Germans dominant. As a child whenever I did anything "wrong", the first admonition was "shame on you." As I grew older the common refrain was, "If people only knew you as I do, they would know how horrible you are." Of course, these things were said in anger and frustration, but as a child, these words and the energy behind them were deeply absorbed not only in my psyche but also in the core energy structure of my body. As I struggled with these demons, my mother, for the most part, continued to be loving and appreciative towards me. I doubt if she remembered the harsh and hurtful things that she said to me in my childhood, nor the intense anger behind them. She was a Midwestern mother in the fifties at a time when her identity was dependent on having the perfect home, the perfect marriage and the perfect children. I am sure that she felt it was her job to mold me into a proper young lady befitting that time period. I doubt that it was her intention to attempt to control and alter my basic nature, but as a child it felt that way. Yet as I spent more time with her, her unhappiness at her life situation and my inability to make things better evoked these feelings. I slowly watched as my energy field was pulled into the gray heavy, judgmental field of my ancestry, and the place and time in which I grew up.

Teachings from the Retreat

During the retreat, we learned practices that burn off and remove blocks to our well-being while streaming in healing energy from the divine. The Red Garuda is a mythical being from the divine frequency realm that is part-man and part-bird. He simultaneously pulls down energy from the divine realm for healing while burning away obstacles in and around us on the physical plane. A powerful deity, the Garuda eradicates obstacles and heals simultaneously. For him to work effectively, one must clearly set one's intention and request his help. Through chanting and prayer, he comes to work with us. The first day of the retreat I was consumed with what the Buddhists call *small mind*. It is the mind of mundane details and empty thoughts and musings such as "What should I wear tomorrow" or "I wonder why the person in front of me is chanting so loudly," anything to pull me from myself and the deep holding of the inner refuge. As I began to corral my untamed mind and come to a place of peace, the painful feelings of shame and unworthiness arose. I feared that the hundred plus people in the meditation hall could see and sense the negative energy that had engulfed me. At the breaks, it was difficult for me to look at others. I had not allowed myself to consider that others in the hall were experiencing their own demons as we all released negative energies from our energy fields.

As the retreat progressed, the negative feelings began to dissipate and I could feel the joy and peace to which I had been accustomed return to fill my being. I now understand that the painful feelings that were present at the beginning of the retreat had become so prominent within my consciousness and energy body in order to rise up to be released and healed. I am so grateful for the wisdom of the Tibetans and to Rinpoche for their willingness to bring these sacred teachings to the West.[3] This form of healing work is not an easy magical cure as many in the West long for. It calls upon each of us to face the full force of our pain and suffering before it can be released. By the end of the retreat I felt free of these heavy and painful energies. Layers of childhood crud had lifted so that I could feel the brilliance of the divine realms flow through. In this freedom, I have been able to reflect on the power of these early energies to engulf and shape who we are.

The Energy Within and Without

For decades, psychotherapists have tried to define what it is that propels clients to actually make a life-altering shift. If it were as simple as understanding why we feel and act the way we do, we would all be happy and healed in six to eight psychotherapy sessions as most talented therapists can divine this understanding within a brief time frame; but clearly this is not the case as those who have been in psychotherapy can attest. The assertion that we can achieve true happiness if we merely change our outlook does not always bring life-altering change either. Most of us have experienced moods or energies that swarm over us in an all-pervasive way that we do not fully understand nor know how to alter. There is a variety of meditation and energetic techniques such as yoga, Chi Kung and Tai Chi that help to shift stuck and unpleasant energies, but patterns and imprints that are deeply embedded in our fields are not so easily released.

Many have been inspired by *The Secret*[4] and the channeled work of Abraham-Hicks.[5] In these teachings, we have been taught that what we think will draw to us that which we envision; it is called the law of attraction. If we believe that we will do poorly in a job interview, the energy of the belief will be dominant and we will most likely have a rough time in the interview and not get the job. Conversely if we go to the interview feeling confident and at ease, envisioning ourselves getting the job, this energy will bring the results that we desire. There is infinite wisdom in these teachings; it is a fundamental tenet of the shamanic teachings that I received from my teacher, Ismail Daim. Ismail, known as the Bomoh, said that when one focuses the mind while consulting with spiritual guides and teachers, the combined intention of these forces can alter the energy field around us and, as a healer, alter the energy field in others. The Bomoh taught me that when I heal another, I need to hold the intention of what is to occur and to hold this intention until the healing is complete. If I am working with someone who has a broken heart, I hold the intention of the heart healing as I am guided by my power animals and spirit guides as to how to heal the broken heart. If I am working with someone who has cancerous cells in the body, then I hold the intention of these cells transforming to healthy, cancer-free cells.

Riding the wave of positive intentions enables us to manifest what we desire. The challenge, however, is staying in the wave of the positive. It is possible to hold these intentions around certain tasks or desires, but to hold one's intention 24/7 with all of the distractions of the modern world and unhealed aspects of our being is a herculean task even for the most seasoned practitioner. Many are still encased in energies from our past that make it a struggle to stay on top of the wave no matter how hard we will it. It is as if there are 30-pound weights attached to our feet as we struggle to stay afloat. Fortunately, there are ways to remove and heal these weights, but first we must acknowledge that they are there and have the courage to face the painful effect that may emerge.

Second, we must not blame ourselves for the weights being there but view the healing of these burdens as an opportunity, a gift. One of my clients, Heather, who is a devotee of the Abraham-Hicks teachings, was diagnosed with cancer. As she told me of the diagnosis, she began to sob. The first words out of her mouth were, "What have I done wrong?" The belief that we create our own realities meant that she had created her cancer. Through journey work we learned that the cancer was part of the stuck and unhealed energy from her mother's side of the family. The cancer was in the throat area; the area of the fifth chakra[6] which governs expression of what is truly in the heart. There had been secrets on her mother's side of the family. Heather had grown up feeling censored, believing that she could only speak that which was acceptable to her mother. The energy of censorship had grown a small tumor as a way of alerting Heather to this repressed energy. It was there so that it could be cleared and healed. In removing and healing the stuck energy, the healing was not just for Heather, but for her mother, her sister and all in their lineage who felt censored or acted from a place of censorship. When the energy was removed, I envisioned it transforming into a sparkling array of stars that were full of healing light and freedom. These stars were shared not only with Heather but with others in her family; some of whom are on the physical plane, while others are on the spiritual plane. When there is a healing to transform and release harmful ancestral or karmic imprints, the healing is not just for the individual carrying the energy but for all who are or have been connected to the imprints. The goal is to free as many as possible from the debilitating energies that block us from connection to our true essence, our true heart.

I too went through layers of self-judgment when the painful effect from my childhood arose. I had spent years in therapy, meditation and in work with my guides and believed that the energy states which arose during the retreat were healed; how dare these feelings reemerge! I have an arsenal of healing practices to use, yet none could dent the effective layer of negative self-judgment and confusion that arose from this entrenched ancestral imprint. I began to question not only myself, but also the efficacy of what I had been taught. How could I convince others of the veracity of our abilities to heal ourselves if it did not work for me? I now realize that our healing is rarely complete. As a layer of pain and suffering is cleared there are deeper levels that rise to the surface to be understood and cleared when the opportune moment arises as we gradually open to our true essence, who we truly are.

As has been the case throughout my training as a shamanic practitioner, spirit provides me with the lessons that I need to deepen my work to the next level of healing and understanding. Usually spirit guides bestow their wisdom to me through my work with clients. I am constantly challenged with situations that on first glance leave me feeling clueless as to what is going on or what to do, and yet, like magic, they bring light and clarity as to what I am to do for a true healing to occur. This time the teaching was personal, but sorely needed for my own healing as well as for the healing of others.

For several years I have been aware of the power of ancestral and karmic imprints, and used extraction and energy work to heal these imprints in my work with others. But it was not until I experienced the full force of an ancestral imprint did I realize what is truly involved in the release of these energies. We must have the courage to sit in the muck of feeling states that were too painful to digest and process as children. As children, we rarely had the support needed or even the full awareness of what was happening to us to understand or work with these feelings. Instead we dissociated from them and/or built defenses to protect ourselves from further harm. These defenses served us well when we were young, but the barriers that we erected then, now stand in the way of our healing. In order to have the courage to face feelings that felt unbearable when we were little, we need to feel accompanied by the holding of another presence that loves, accepts, and embraces us in this process. This is why I believe that shamanic work, be it from the ancient teachings of the Bön, an indigenous shaman, or contemporary shamanism, is extremely helpful in the healing and transformation of the energetic imprints that we bravely bring to the light for release.

Path to Healing Ancestral Imprints

Tenzin Wangyal Rinpoche built a powerful energy field, strong enough to hold each of us in the initial painful days of our shedding. As the retreat went on, the positive energy of over a hundred people chanting was truly amazing. We not only focused on ourselves but on others that were in need of healing with particular focus on the pain and suffering of those at Virginia Tech.

When I experienced the lifting of my childhood imprint of shame and unacceptability, my mother also experienced a healing as well. Undoubtedly, she carried the energy of shame in her field as well as a finely programmed view as to what was acceptable behavior in a small child. These energies with their accompanying beliefs stemmed from her experiences as a child and those of her parents before. As I concentrated on this energy dissolving during the retreat, I pictured it disintegrating from both my mother's and my field and from all in our lineage that were affected as well. I saw the web of negative energy burn away and the harmful energetic pattern between us evaporate. Yes, there are still moments when I can feel the pull of this negative energy. It occurs primarily when I am tired or not fully in my heart. This patterning is deeply embedded in the psyche, but the energy that holds it there is healed. When the negative thoughts arise, I note them and ask my guides to help me to release rather than grow these thoughts as we all often do by the constant retelling of a story of a negative experience in our thoughts. The relationship between my mother and myself remained in a positive, loving place until her death; this enabled me to care for her without guilt or recrimination; the traces of the shameful energy appear to have evaporated. As the end of my mother's life approached, it was apparent to both of us that love, compassion, understanding and forgiveness are at the core of our lives no matter the belief systems that encapsulate these views. The universality of certain truths overrides parochial thought forms and brings us closer to our true hearts.

Many from the baby boomer generation found our values, politics and lifestyle at odds with parents who had confronted a Great Depression, a terrifying war and longed for nothing more than normality and conformity. Many of my generation found the push for projecting normality and conformity stifling and, at times, inauthentic. I chose an incarnation in which I grew up in a conservative Midwestern town in the 50s and a path that took me to a remote village in Malaysian Borneo to study ancient healing practices. My guides directed me to forge an integration of an ancient indigenous shamanic practice with contemporary psychological thought in order to bring healing to the wounded Western psyche. To accomplish my life work I was required to go against many of the deeply held beliefs and customs from my childhood, culture and professional training. As a child, I felt shocked and betrayed when my mother tried to stifle and corral the essence that made me who I am. Yet, I imagine that my mother also felt betrayed by my independent spirit that expressed itself in ways which were the antithesis to everything that she believed and spent her life struggling to be. If we had lived together in a different time period where the generational divide was not an issue, perhaps there would not have been a foundation or reason to be in conflict. If we are to reach a new consciousness that is based in acceptance, compassion and an awareness of our interconnection to all that is, we will need to alter the cultural paradigm that views the world in right and wrong thinking encased in judgment and blame to a pattern of belief in which we can see the complexity in each situation and strive to find understanding and compassion rather than judgment and blame. If each time we feel angry, betrayed or hurt by another, we pause to consider the pain that the person hurting us must be in to behave as they are, it might lessen our own hurt and bring us closer to a place of understanding and compassion. Try it, as it can free one from great suffering.

The power of generational beliefs and imprints to shape who we are and why we think and feel the way that we do cannot be underestimated if we are to unravel the many threads that foster disconnection and disagreement. As we step into a global consciousness, a wide array of lifestyles and belief systems are at our fingertips. This is particularly true for those in developing nations where the core rules, rituals and beliefs had been undisturbed for centuries. Many embrace the blending of cultures and feel stimulated by new perspectives in which to view reality. Others feel their life and country threatened by opening to new cultures and new ways of perceiving reality. Much of the strife throughout the world results from countries vying for cultural and economic supremacy. For those who believe that we live many lifetimes, we can consult our internal wisdom to bring to consciousness those incarnations when we were happy and at peace. In doing so we can begin to discern the qualities of living, and the lifestyle, that enabled us to feel joy and peace.

Eckhart Tolle's best-selling book, *A New Earth*,[7] and the profound teachings from contemporary Buddhist teachers skillfully guide us through the steps to release our attention to mind and form so that we can fall into that space where we are one with all. I would not have been able to open to the teachings of the spirit world and all of the wisdom that is available to us if I had not been meditating daily for years. I attended a retreat with renowned Buddhist teacher, Chokyi Nyima. He was teaching on the illusionary nature of mind, gently guiding us to see that what the mind creates is an illusion. At a break I asked for advice as to how to help people work with energy that is in their field from childhood trauma but is not their energy, rather that of those who harmed them. Rinpoche instructed me to tell them to meditate until they see that the energy in their field is an illusion belonging to someone else. It then will be released. This is sage advice for the advanced practitioner, but often I find that it is challenging for a trauma survivor to calm the mind sufficiently to reach this awareness. Often in the calm mind, images of repressed trauma rise up to be released. Unless one is prepared for this and has a skilled teacher to walk with them, these images can be overwhelming and challenging with which to deal. I am grateful for shamanic practices that can extract, heal and transform the energies that are in our field from those who have harmed us.

I have been drawn to shamanism and the Bön Buddhist teachings as they provide a path to both work with the challenging aspects of the mind and the energy in the field that the mind holds in place. Not everyone has the time or inclination to become a meditator. Sometimes we need the skill and expertise of a shamanic or energetic practitioner who has the ability to perceive the energetic imprints in the energy field of another, how to read whose energies might be attached to their client's field, and how to heal, transform and send these healed energies back to its rightful owner. But before this can be successfully done, the client needs to recognize that they are carrying the energy of another and that they cannot be fully whole until those energies are removed and aspects of themselves brought back via a soul retrieval.

If one carries the ancestral imprint of anxiety and fear in her field with an accompanying belief that she is not safe in the world, both the thought form and the energy need to be healed and transformed. Although we live in a time in which the threat of terrorism and violence is ever present, to live in a state of fear of the worst that could happen prevents one from being present to live life, as the fear of what might happen makes the fear a reality in one's life. If we live in fear of what might happen, we are essentially living our life as if what we fear has happened. The most terrifying thing becomes our daily reality. We have to let go of the belief that we are in eminent danger for the fear and anxiety to be released or the mind will just call the energy of fear back—there certainly is enough of free floating fear around to easily absorb the vibration of fear back into our field. Conversely, the anxious energy of fear must be healed, transformed and released, or this energy will invite the belief that one is unsafe as a way to understand the anxiety and fear racing through the body and energy field. The feeling state beckons to the belief and the belief keeps the feeling state in place. Through working with the imprint of both the belief and the energy of fear and anxiety, we come to understand that safety arises from a place deep within us, not from an external threat or lack thereof.

Psychopomp is the shamanic practice of escorting the dead to the other side. Years ago, I attended a workshop in psychopomp with a Lapland shaman named Ailo Gaup. During the workshop Ailo led us on a shamanic journey in which we died and went to the other side. Before we did the journey, we were asked to write on a piece of paper that we promised to come back. At first I thought this odd, but once I did the journey I understood why. When I left my body to go to the other side, there were deceased loved ones there to greet me. At first I saw them in a holographic form, but soon they were mere energy vibrations, yet I intuitively knew who they were and connected with them. The feeling state was total bliss as I merged into a consciousness of peace and love with other energy beings around me. In that instance I knew that this was home and I relaxed into a sense of calm and well-being. When the drumbeat changed to call us back, I did not want to return. Although I was quite happy in my life on earth, I wanted to stay. I forced myself to return, however, knowing that I had made a commitment to be on the earth at this time and that I had much more work to do. Most importantly this experience awakened within me the awareness of our collective consciousness coupled with the peace and well-being that comes from being one with all that is. With this understanding, any fears that I had regarding safety on the planet dissipated.

If we allow ourselves to open to a more expansive way of viewing reality, we can shed cultural imprints that tell us what to think and how to be, ancestral imprints that carry both the pain and gifts of our ancestors, and come to better understand more thoroughly the influence that our previous lifetimes have on who we are. In the spaciousness of these new perspectives there is room for who we truly are to emerge. It is easy, however, in this concrete material world to lose touch with the spiritual nature of our existence and to become attached to all of the activities and material possessions that we believe we need to be happy. In order for us to create a world in which we can live in peace and understanding, we need to rid ourselves of our attachment to those things large and mundane that keep us from our true heart; allow the challenging energies that we carry from our ancestors and our previous incarnations to be healed, released, and transformed; and without an attachment to ego believe that we have the power and the wisdom to create the world in which we want to live.

Chapter 4

From Madness to Peace

I was at the cabin in Vermont working on this book. After a couple of days of isolated writing, I ventured out to the hardware store to get a few things. I turned on the radio to hear Mahatma Gandhi's grandson, Arun Gandhi, speak on NPR's program, An Alternative Life. *I smiled knowing that there are no accidents. He quoted his grandfather as stating that he was not afraid to die for his beliefs, that was not a concern for him, but that there was nothing that was worth doing violence over. Arun Gandhi went on to say that trying to negotiate for peace while waging war is like putting out a fire with equal parts water and gasoline. Before we can have peace, we must work with the anger that we feel in our hearts.*

We live in a time of war, hostility, prejudice and fear. With nuclear stockpiles housed throughout the world, we have the potential to blow up the planet many times over. Although we long for peace and tranquility, we often feel powerless to impact the bellicose rhetoric that threatens our adversaries and urges us to hate and distrust anyone who is different from us. Before we can successfully sue for peace, we must first come to understand and work with the anger that lies in wait in our energy fields for expression and discharge that we have absorbed from our ancestors, previous incarnations and from the culture at large. Once we come to understand how to identify and work with our negative energetic states, we will no longer be held captive by them. As we shift our collective vibrational fields from anger and fear to compassion and understanding, we can begin to create a world that is at peace. We grasp the concept of trending when a wave of interest in a topic takes off and it becomes the new best thing. Energetically we do the same thing. A kind and open heart can shift the energy in a room of conflict, quickly spreading to others as more and more people seek consensus and understanding just as the energetic power of an angry mob can ignite violence and entice people to act in an uncharacteristically horrific manner.

Before I studied and worked as a shamanic practitioner, my professional practice as a clinical psychologist specialized in treating those who had suffered from traumatic experiences. I was drawn to shamanic work as a result of witnessing the destructive energetic power of physical, sexual and psychic abuse from one person to another. I watched in suppressed horror as a client's body reenacted an unthinkable trauma that violently forced to consciousness the buried memory of incredible pain and suffering. One young woman hemorrhaged mid-cycle with severe cramping for several days. Then intrusive and unrelenting images arose, which gradually revealed that her father had taken her to an alleged doctor when she was eleven to abort his child. Energetically the body had held the physical and emotional pain of this experience—pain so great that the psyche had no choice but to suppress it from conscious memory.

As I listened to her experience and witnessed the pain in both her body and soul, anger filled me with a blind rage towards the father who would do this to his little girl. Although I did not share this anger with her, I knew that, in part, I was feeling some of the anger that my client could not allow herself to feel in her traumatized frightened place. I also knew that some of it was mine. As I conjured up violent fantasies about the father, I tried to call on compassion for his tortured soul, for the father who must have been incredibly wounded to do such things to his daughter. I tried to be mindful that my own anger only serves to grow the vibration of anger, the desire to do harm or seek revenge in a world that is inundated with this negative vibration.

After the session, I allowed myself to feel the full force of the anger, to sit and be with it realizing that energetic vibrations from my own childhood had been activated. In being with the anger I was able to bear witness to it and then release it. If I had tried to push it down, it would have gone back into my body only to be reactivated again. I reminded myself of the importance of holding both the anger and the compassion for the incredible pain that one must be in to harm one's child in such a hideous manner.

My entire life I have tried to understand, as many of us have, why it is that man can act so cruelly to one another, why there is such suffering in the world and such an imbalance in material goods and standard of living throughout the world. The notion of a wrathful and punishing God never resonated with my felt sense of a divine and loving force in the universe. Nor did the strict interpretation of karma, which asserts that what we sow in one lifetime, we will reap in the next, as this only serves to blame those who live lives of suffering for their plight. Nor was I willing to accept that at our core we are all sinners, condemned by Eve's disobedience. These rigid interpretations of Eastern and Western religions seem to miss the essence of the love, acceptance, and compassion that was at the heart of the message of the great teachers in whose name these religions came into being.

Through reading, discussion, but most importantly from teachings from my guides, I came to an ever-evolving understanding. We come from and return to a divine energy, but for reasons that are unclear, we have chosen to be incarnate on the physical plane. Before we cycle off this planet to reunite with the divine, we must experience everything that there is to experience on the physical plane.[8] Thus if we have not yet experienced the ravages of war and genocide, we will. Just as we each will have a turn to be rich and famous. Our source of empathy undoubtedly stems from the experiences that we have had in other lifetimes. These experiences compel us to confront the complexities of a situation rather than stay in the dualistic thinking of right and wrong.

As we live more and more lifetimes, we gather wisdom and

compassion while simultaneously carrying the energetic burdens of the pain that we have caused and endured. Most of us at one time or another have felt angry enough to want to harm or to see someone harmed in some way. If we have felt this way, or perhaps even done this in another lifetime, we are more likely to have compassion for someone who commits a crime of passion. Concurrently we are more likely to control our own destructive impulses when we carry an awareness of the enormous burden of acting from blind rage. Embedded in our energy field is the destructive, vengeful impulse which we carry from our ancestral, cultural and karmic imprints that is also tempered with wisdom and compassion. These competing energies vie for dominance as we aspire to bring forth our better selves. As we enter a new age of awareness and expansion, we are blessed with the ability to heal the negative energies that reside within our energy field, to shed the ancestral and karmic burdens while embracing the gifts and lessons that we have received over our many lifetimes. Historically one of the roles of shamans was to keep in balance the competing forces of evil and goodness. Since the beginning of the 21st century, my spirit guides have stressed that as we enter a new era of consciousness, the light or positive forces will begin to absorb, heal and transform the negative forces on the planet. The Bomoh stressed in his teachings that the divine forces are much more powerful than the destructive ones, and that the divine light can heal and transform the negative destructive forces that haunt us.

According to my spirit guides, we come into each of our lifetimes with a karmic lesson or wound to heal as well as a plan or a purpose of what we are to manifest in this incarnation. Thus the circumstances of our birth and the experiences in our childhood most often contain some aspect of what we came here to heal and what we came here to be. For some this philosophy is hard to comprehend as they have endured such suffering in their early lives that they cannot fathom that this is something that they would have chosen. I have struggled with this construct myself. But it is from this struggle that I feel compelled to write this book, to speed the soul's journey from a place of suffering to one of wholeness by offering ways to unburden the soul of the ancestral, cultural and karmic baggage that we carry.

Energetically and vibrationally we carry both unhealed energies from previous incarnations, our ancestors, and the cultural, racial, generational and spiritual imprints from our current incarnation. At our core is a pure soul essence that is layered with these various vibrations and energies. Through shamanic work the unhealed energies of our karmic and ancestral imprints can be healed, transformed and released. But first there is work to be done to prepare oneself for this release; work that must be done with the utmost care and compassion.

If we can imagine that this particular lifetime is merely one phase of our soul's journey, like being in the third grade, and that there is much to learn and experience both in this lifetime and in others, it lessens the impact of the challenging emotions that must be confronted. Often we feel enormous shame and embarrassment for shadow energies that we carry, holding onto them as precious nuggets of coal. It is difficult for the Western mind to comprehend the transitory and energetic base of these energies and the lessons that we have chosen to learn by having them. One of the most difficult emotions to contend with is the hurt, anger and resentment that we feel towards those who have harmed us. Depending on our childhood experiences and the vibrational imprints that we carry from other lifetimes, we may suppress these feelings, choose to act them out in passive aggressive ways, or strike out trying to wound as we were wounded.

In many healing practices it is deemed important to recognize, identify and work with our feelings before they can be released. If we try to ignore, repress or rise above them, they can go into the body only to reappear as illness. In psychotherapy, one is accompanied and supported while these difficult feelings are confronted. In this safe context it is possible to remember and process prior traumas in the safety of another's care providing the support that was so sorely missing during the initial traumas.

Sadly some stay stuck in these hurt, angry feelings and become energetically encased in them through the constant retelling of the traumas. The core identity becomes that of a trauma victim. All too many become frozen in this phase of the healing process and never come to see who they truly are. As we gradually let go of the anger and resentment towards those who have harmed us, we begin to see these experiences as teachings for our soul's process and growth. From this state it is possible to free ourselves from the negative energy states that bind us to those who harmed us. Anger and hate keep us energetically connected to another just as powerfully as love does. Stuck anger stops us from experiencing the peace that comes from settling into our true heart as we are constantly doing battle with the other, keeping the memory and the energy of the trauma alive. After the tragic murder of nine people during a Bible study session at Emanuel African Methodist church in Charleston, South Carolina, the parishioners were able to offer heartfelt forgiveness to Dylann Roof. In doing this, they were able to grieve in a state of peace rather than from a rage that would haunt them.

As in most things, there needs to be balance. One cannot rush to forgiveness and acceptance before one is ready as then the feelings are submerged only to arise once more. But it is essential that we are able to see the trauma as something that happened to us rather than who we are. In the process of doing shamanic healing work for trauma survivors, and let's face it most of us have experienced some form of wounding, the energy of the trauma cannot be released and healed if the personality views the trauma as the core of who they are.

Working with the Western Psyche

There are challenges for those who were born or educated in Western cultures that those who live more closely connected to spirit do not encounter. The Western psyche is quite complex and grounded in the intricacies of the material world. The influence of the Christian-Judea religion coupled with the philosophies of Descartes and Newton have produced a materialistic and dualistic frame of reference, which narrows the way in which we perceive the world and how we fit into the grander scheme of things. As a result of inherent intellectual and cultural imprints that influence our way of thinking, it is often difficult for the Western mind to conceptualize an energy body, let alone release those things housed in the energy body that no longer belong. It is equally challenging to grasp that we are accompanied by guides, teachers and power animals that energetically surround us and are here to teach, guide and protect us.

There are cultures in which shamanism and shamanic practices are at the vibrational and cognitive center of the culture. When I first lived in Matu, Western medicine was a scary and harmful practice; most shunned all aspects of it with the exception of Band-Aids, which they concretely could see were helpful. Thus it was very easy to do shamanic work there as there were no cultural or psychological blocks to working with energy and with guides. From my years of doing shamanic work in the West, however, I have become aware that there are several steps involved before the energetic baggage that we carry can be fully released energetically.

Our psychic processes are quite complex. We tend to take quite seriously all the myriad thoughts that float through our minds; we often treat our thoughts as fact. It is the beliefs or thought forms that hold the harmful ancestral and karmic energies in place. Identifying a non-productive thought form and understanding our attachments to this belief is the first step. It is important to understand that we did not consciously create self-defeating beliefs and energies, but that we absorbed, inherited or created them to explain things that seemed unexplainable. When we tell ourselves that we will never have the job of our dreams, where does that voice come from? Did our teachers or parents limit us with these words? Did we perceive others as having an easier time of getting ahead and decide to quit trying? Is this a belief that is carried throughout our ancestral lineage? Did our parents and grandparents pass on the myth that our family never gets ahead? Or is this a deeply held belief from our experiences in other lifetimes? Did we receive messages from the culture at large that if we are a minority or female we will never achieve the success that white males can? The origin of the belief is not as important as the fact that we imbue it with the veracity of a concrete reality. In the abstract we can all agree that this is a self-limiting belief that is not a fact, but when it exists in our own mind, it often feels like fact. One of my favorite bumper stickers simply states: "Don't believe everything that you think."

Second, we need to comprehend the degree to which we have been shadowboxing these energies throughout our lifetime. These unhealed energies and beliefs lie in wait in our energy field and in our psyche for the perfect opportunity for healing and then they pop out much like an unwanted pimple. We are feeling happy and confident. Then we encounter a person that has a look or a tone of a teacher who regularly shattered our confidence. Our habitual response to the teacher's negative provocation was to act out in some way that verified that we were indeed a no good fool. Before we are even aware of the trigger, we are acting unaccustomedly like we did in the 7th grade. The feelings of inadequacy and embarrassment flood our being as we stand there wondering what just happened. It had been years since we acted in such a boorish manner and re-experienced the feelings of shame and self-doubt that were deeply buried inside from our childhood. Yet these feelings often haunted us in the dream state and unconsciously have held us back from truly standing in our power. They had been lurking around waiting for an opportunity to surface so that they could be healed and released. We are no longer the defiant acting-out 13 year old, but the feelings from that time period have been held shamefully in our field.

Third, it is necessary to let go of the stories that we tell ourselves about these negative imprints. These stories encase us energetically in the event; as a result, a part of us remains behind and lives frozen there. Some of us continually grow stories from our past in which we are the victim of another's cruel actions. We tell anyone who will listen how badly we were treated. Proudly we wear the cloak of victimization, and by doing so energetically draw to us more and more negative experiences of the same ilk. I am in no way suggesting that we blame the victim for their own victimization, but rather try to bring to light the energetic base of how our thoughts, beliefs and stories can keep the pain of our trauma deeply embedded in our energy field. As a result, we energetically draw that which we do not want to us. Conversely, some choose to take the full weight of another's negative treatment as proof of our core badness. "If I was not a despicable human being, my father would not have raped and beaten me." As long as we stay ensconced in the stories of how horrible people have treated us or what a dreadful person we are, we will continue to draw more people to us that treat us in the way that fits our negative life story. This is the law of attraction at work in the negative pole.

Whether we blame ourselves, the other, or both, we are stuck in the energy of blame and from this place it is difficult to heal. I have found from my many years of doing psychotherapy and shamanic work that no one can deeply heal until they are able to develop compassion for themselves and all that they went through and, in time, come to a place of understanding as to why the person that harmed us did so. Thus the fourth step is to let go of the blame and thank the experience for the opportunity to grow and heal this negative imprint. The energy of blame stems from the dualistic perspective of right and wrong. Either I am right or they are right. It assumes that the other set out to intentionally harm us, that there are no extenuating circumstances to explain why the other acted as they did. I doubt if there are many parents that intentionally have a child for the purpose of seeing what harm they can do to them. Rather they project their own pain and wounds onto their child thereby perceiving the child as the worst version of themselves; one that deserves to be beaten and verbally abused.

One of my clients, Judy, is the survivor of both incest and church ritual abuse. Her father had sexually abused her from the time she was a baby. When Judy was seven, her father took her to a priest for an exorcism. As her father watched, the priest and three "assistants" ritually tortured and raped her in order to rid her of the demon, the evil inside, that caused her father to rape her. Unfortunately, the exorcism did not work, as her father continued to rape her. As we gasp in shock at the full horror of this accounting, it is difficult not to feel enraged at the priest, the father, and a misogynist church for what they did. Without question, they should be held to account for their actions and, sadly, all too often they are not. Yet I urge you to explore with me the complexity of the situation in order to find understanding and the opportunity for growth and change.

Judy spent most of her adult life convinced that there was evil inside of her; how could one not after such a dehumanizing attack in which she was repeatedly told she was in fact evil by both her father and her priest. A focus of the therapy was to shift and heal this perspective. Judy struggled to grasp that what they did was wrong, that she had done nothing to deserve this horrendous treatment. A major challenge in healing her deeply held conviction in her own culpability was the belief that if she was not evil, then her father, the priest and his assistants were. Despite what her father did to her, a part of her loved him and was loyal to him, just as a part of her had strong religious beliefs. Unable to accept that what they had done to her was cruel and depraved, she went back to claiming the evil as her own.

It was only through acceptance of the enormous amount of trauma and pain that her father must have experienced to do the things that he did that Judy was able to move out of the belief that she was evil. The dualistic paradigm in the West which asserts that one is either good or bad was the stumbling block to her healing; if something is amiss, then someone must be to blame. She was not evil, nor was her father. Rather he was deeply wounded and felt great guilt for his actions or he would not have taken her to church for the exorcism. Unable to accept responsibility for his actions, he convinced himself that it was her evilness that "made" him rape her. When most likely, he had also been abused and felt compelled to rid himself of this abuse by abusing the one he loved the most.

It had not been possible to heal and remove the energetic web of the trauma, self-hate and woundedness that bound them both until Judy was able to let go of the belief that she was evil and deserved the horrendous treatment which she had endured. Once she grasped that she was not evil, but rather the victim of soul-shattering abuse, the removal of her father's disturbing energy as well as the abhorrent energy from the ritual abuse perpetrated by a priest in the name of God was crucial. Just as beliefs or thought forms can call negative energy into one's energy field, negative energy in one's field prompts the mind to find a reason to explain the painful leaden energy, thereby inducing a cycle of negative beliefs and energetic states.

Given the amount of trauma from rape and ritual abuse stored in Judy's energy field and body as well as destructive and wounded energy her father, the priest and his minions left behind, it took time to remove all of these destructive energetic states as there were layers upon layers of trauma. Once Judy understood the full extent of what had been done to her, she was eager to rid herself of this energy. In removing energy from one's field, it is important to fill the vacuum with positive healed energy. Each time that Judy was sexually assaulted, she dissociated. In psychological terms this means that she lost conscious awareness of what was happening to her and had no clear memory of it afterwards. It can be ten, twenty or even thirty years or more before one has glimpses of what happened. From a shamanic perspective, when one is traumatized part of one's soul essence leaves and the energy of the trauma and/or the energy of the perpetrator rushes in to fill the void. Thus, an extraction of the energy must be performed coupled with a soul retrieval. When the energy of another is extracted, it must be healed and returned to the person to whom it belongs. Often in acts of violence, not only does the perpetrator leave part of his energy behind, but he also takes the energy of the one he is harming. In Judy's case, her father had a great deal of her soul essence and this needed to be retrieved and healed. Even if this person has died, as was the case with Judy's father, healed parts of his soul essence can be returned to him to assist in his soul's evolution while simultaneously Judy's energy is retrieved. It is not possible to return energy to someone without removing energy in the field that is not one's own; it is a basic principle of physics.

In addition to healing from her father's abuse, Judy actively struggled to understand and heal the institutionally sanctioned violence that she experienced by members of her church. She became an activist and leader in the clergy abuse scandal in Boston working hard to both confront and heal what had happened to all of those who had been sexually and ritually abused by the clergy. Institutionally sanctioned torture and violence is a complex topic that is addressed later as we attempt to understand and unburden ourselves not only from the karmic and cultural burdens that we carry as individuals, but also as members of larger communities and institutions.

The last step in healing both emotionally and energetically is to develop compassion and forgiveness for all that we have done and for those who have harmed us. This simple tenet is at the foundation of the major religions in the world, yet it seems that the Old Testament sentiment of "an eye for an eye and a tooth for a tooth" is the belief that most live by. From a purely energetic perspective, we are connected to those we hate in the same way we are connected to those we love as the energy of hate binds us together just as the energy of love does. Strong energy that emanates from the heart, be it positive or negative, keeps us vibrationally connected. Most have had the experience of meeting someone to whom we have an initial negative reaction for no apparent reason. Often these are people with whom we have unresolved conflict from other lifetimes. Sometimes the need to heal and resolve the conflict is so strong that we incarnate in the same family compelling us to deal with one another. Unless our differences are addressed and forgiven in this lifetime, we may reenact the same harmful dynamics from one lifetime to the next.

From both personal and professional experience, a state of forgiveness and understanding cannot be obtained before we are ready. If we rush to forgiveness before we fully feel and experience forgiveness deeply in our heart, the feelings of anger and hurt go underground resulting in depression or physical illness. If, however, we set the intention of reaching a state of understanding and acceptance, rather than one of blame and revenge, we pave the way for an energetic shift that allows for deep healing and clearing.

If we can embrace the hurtful and traumatic experiences in our lives as teachings for the evolution and growth of our soul, the healing process will go more smoothly. The energy of hate, resentment and anger, emotions that must be felt and experienced in the early stages of healing trauma and abuse, must eventually give way to acceptance and understanding if the energetic bond between the victim and perpetrator is to be broken and healed. If the angry bond remains in full force, then one is frozen in the energy of the trauma and is unable to move on to experience peace and joy in one's life.

Spiraling Energy

As each of us walks into a more peaceful heart, this energy radiates out and shifts the vibration on the planet. This was felt quite palpably after the election of Barack Obama. There was a profound sense of hope and promise that accompanied his campaign and election. From America's inception, the ugly mantel of racism and genocide has been a dark mark on the collective psyche and energy field of all who have lived within its borders. Even those who did not vote for Obama reported feeling happy, even relieved, that the deeply embedded racial attitudes in the United States had shifted sufficiently for an African American to be elected president. Despite being in the midst of one of the worst economic crises in the nation's history, the majority of Americans were said to feel optimistic. The deeply held desire of those who aspired to embrace "our better angels" had a leader and a movement to embrace and grow this yearning and, most importantly, inspire us to obtain it. The wish to be a country that worked together rather than at odds with one another, that fostered understanding rather than hate and fear, elected a leader that espoused these values. With Obama's election, the collective energy field of the nation appeared to be on the verge of shifting.

Sadly those who clung to the politics and beliefs of the past countered with anger, hate, and a level of obstructionism that forced them to alter positions they had deeply held so as to not to be in agreement with the President. The undercurrent of racism that had been submerged below the surface raised its ugly head through the Birther Movement that asserted that President Obama was not a US citizen despite documented proof to the contrary. The Birther Movement, created by Donald Trump, sought to thrust us back to an earlier time when the white patriarchal structure was intact. Eight years later, Trump cultivated the shadow or negative aspect of our collective nature by running an anti-immigrant, anti-Muslim and anti-woman campaign that propelled him to the presidency. Given the energetic shifts that are occurring on the planet, it is understandable that some would find the press for racial, gender, economic and cultural equality uncomfortable and would endeavor to find their footing by attempting to re-create a time in which they felt safe, a time when white men ruled and women, racial and cultural minorities knew their place.

The whiplash from one extreme to the next underlies the importance of understanding and examining the extent to which we can be carried along in the wave of the collective energy field with energies that run counter to what we truly feel. The energy behind both Obama's and Trump's rise to power was the desire for change. Initially, it was a desire and hope for change in a positive, cooperative and kind manner. When that change was blocked, the collective frustration that ensued brought to power a bombastic leader who desired to radically change everything.

Before we can explore how these energies shifted in the collective, it is important to understand where they live within us individually. If the thread of racism that vibrationally lives in each of us from our ancestral, karmic and cultural imprints had been eradicated, then the Birther Movement would not have obtained a foothold in the American psyche. Take a moment to think back to your childhood and the messages that you received growing up regarding race, gender, class and culture. The extremely popular television series, *Mad Men*, brilliantly captured the culture of the 50s and 60s. Many baby boomers reported being mesmerized by the show as it brought them back to their lives as children. White men had all of the power and women were valued for their attractiveness and sexual appeal rather than their skills and talents. People of color rarely appeared on the show, and when they did, were stereotypically portrayed as befitting the time period. I remember the messages that I received growing up: Native Americans were called Indians, or, even worse, savages; I was told never to let a boy think that I was smarter or a better athlete than he was. In addition I was advised to be kind to "colored people", but not to touch them. I found this hard to comprehend as my beloved babysitter, who was African American, often held and comforted me. The dominant message of my childhood was to be wary of people who are "other than us". Growing up in the Midwest, I was even taught that "others" included people on the East Coast as they allegedly had no morals and were communists. Each of us can recite bizarre and even humorous things we were taught as children that we have had to unlearn as the times changed. I saw *Dances with Wolves* with my mother. Afterward she revealed that she was surprised to see that Native Americans were not that different from us as they seemed to love their families just as we do, that they were not really the savages that she had been taught. Perhaps the multi-generational attempt to dehumanize Native Americans served to salve the collective guilt over the genocide of the original inhabitants of North America.

We can change our beliefs about a group of people and see them in a more just and humane way, but the fear of the other is another matter as the fear lives in our energetic body. Shamefully, but instinctively, I have clutched my bag tighter to my body as an "other" approached me on the street. The "other" has changed throughout the years from Native Americans to African Americans, Hispanics and Muslims, and yes, even women. Sadly the fear of the other has been used to successfully manipulate us, to divide the working and middle class against one another so we will ignore what the ruling class is doing. We must monitor those spontaneous energetic reactions, notice when they arise, and breathe into them with the intent of understanding and releasing them. If we allow the energetic traces of hate and racism to lie dormant in our energy field without owning and recognizing that they are there, we can be swept into the energetic wave of a movement that on a cognitive level we do not actually believe. Many women, working class people and minorities vote against their own self-interest with an underlying and unprocessed sense that someone who is from "our group" could not be a good leader. Internalized sexism, racism and classism are held both cognitively and energetically. The first step is to acknowledge that they are there.

The land also holds the energetic imprint of what occurred upon it. Many make pilgrimages to sacred holy sites in order to absorb the positive, loving and healing energy of the land. Others can sense the dank dark energies of places where great suffering ensued. Fortunately there are energetic practices that can clear trauma from a battlefield or the place where a murder has transpired. It is more challenging to clear the energetic imprint of genocide and enslavement from the land as it is so all-pervasive and covers such a vast amount of land. The first step, understandably, is in acknowledging that it is there.

Wesley Clark Jr., a war veteran and noted author and spokesman, accompanied a group of veterans to Standing Rock in North Dakota to join Native Americans in protest over a pipeline that was to be built through sacred Native American land. Mr. Clark knelt in front of the Native American leaders and said the following:

We came here to be the conscience of the nation. And within that conscience, we must first confess our sins to you, because many of us, me in particular, are from the units that have hurt you over the many years. We came. We fought you. We took your land. We signed treaties that we broke. We stole minerals from your sacred hills. We blasted the faces of our presidents onto your sacred mountain. When we took still more land, and then we took your children, then we tried to take your language, and we tried to eliminate your language that God gave you and that the Creator gave you, we didn't respect you. We polluted your earth.

The veterans began to kneel as Wesley Clark Jr. concluded his statement:

We've hurt you in so many ways, but we've come to say that we are sorry, we are at your service, and we beg for your forgiveness.

This is a beautiful step in the right direction, but so much more is needed to heal the United States of the energetic imprint of genocide and the brutality of slavery. Until the nation as a whole is ready to make a heartfelt apology for our sins and the sins of our ancestors, make amends to those we harmed and begin to respect the sacredness of the earth upon which we live, the deleterious energies that live within the land from these abhorrent practices will commingle with the energy of hate and fear that imprison us and keep us from our true hearts.

In order to rid the world of the madness of war, hate and suffering, we must first eradicate hate and intolerance from our own minds and hearts. What we carry within creates an energy that radiates out and then joins with another's energy; this in turn spirals into energy streams of a similar vibration. If we are intolerant of another's point of view, then we join the energy stream of all beings that are intolerant of those with whom we do not agree. If we strive to see the beauty in each person's heart, then we join the stream of those who look for the beauty in each person. At our core we are all beautiful light beings that have become enshrouded in negative energies from our ancestral, karmic and cultural imprints. Realizing this enables us to shed the negative imprints, embrace the positive ones and live from a gentle and loving heart. One might argue that this is not possible, that it is man's basic nature to be violent. Scattered throughout the world, however, are examples of man's ability to live in peace and respect.

I took a magical trip to Bhutan, a small Himalayan country tucked in between China and India thought by many to be the mythical Shangri-La. Bhutan, the only Himalayan Buddhist country spared from absorption by its powerful neighbors, is a constitutional monarchy.[9] The physical beauty of Bhutan is breathtaking, but this beauty is surpassed by the kindness and gentleness of its people. King Jigme Singye Wangchuck declared the gross national product to be happiness. The Buddhist belief that the sanctity of life extends to all sentient beings, and that we are one with all that is, translates into the most environmentally aware and advanced government on the planet. Cigarettes and plastic are banned. All goods are wrapped in paper or cloth. Eighty percent of the population are farmers. All farming is organic; no chemical fertilizers are used. All of the animals roam freely throughout the countryside, returning home each night to be fed and housed. There is a wildlife preserve that is a seasonal home to the rare and exquisite black-necked crane, a bird that is five to six feet in height. When one of these magnificent birds was tangled up and severely injured by an electric wire, all electric wires in the area of the preserve were taken down and the people were given solar panels.

Life is not perfect in Bhutan. There is suffering and people struggle with issues of poverty, and an inadequate educational and health care system. But there is an inherent difference between the Bhutanese and many other societies. The spiritual and cultural imprint that "we are all one and one with all that is and are part of the infinite consciousness" provides the energetic and cognitive base for the Bhutanese people to experience peace deep within their being. With the understanding that we are all part of the infinite consciousness, there is no need to hate, to fantasize doing harm to another, or for going to war. We are all one and are part of a greater whole. As I travel throughout the world and encounter cultures that are basically peaceful in nature, my belief that our basic nature is loving and kind is confirmed. Perhaps the propensity towards violence and war is culturally determined and not part of our basic nature.

Most aspire to live from the positive aspect of our being, but are often weighed down with the shadow energies of the past. Once we understand and work with the energetic base of our ancestral, cultural, and karmic imprints, we can heal, transform, and release these energies and thought forms and truly become our best selves. As our individual shadow energies are transformed, the collective energy shifts and we move person by person from madness to peace.

Part II

Working with Our Ancestral Imprints

Each of us has an energy body and a dream body that contains vibrational memories of all that has happened to us in this lifetime and in our previous incarnations. In psychological terms, we have an ego or consciousness that remembers certain events and feeling states throughout our lifetime. It occupies a dominant energetic band. There are many occurrences that we do not remember; sometimes because they are insignificant, in other instances they are so upsetting that we split them from conscious memory via a process called dissociation. These forgettable or traumatic events are pushed to the outer edges of one's vibrational field. In addition, we absorb energetic vibrations from our families and the energetic imprints of the culture, while bringing forth the energetic imprints from our previous lifetimes, all of which play an enormous role in how we perceive reality. These various vibrational energies or imprints are constantly intermingling and overlapping with one another. They are holographic, flowing in, out and around our physical and energy bodies. In this section the ancestral imprint will be examined as we unpack both the positive and negative aspects of these imprints, how to grow those that are positive and heal those that are problematic.

Since the beginning of rational or dualistic thinking, there has been a tendency to view people as either good or bad rather than the very complex multilayered people that we are. As we sit primed to enter a new era of consciousness that goes beyond the limitations of dualism, it is important to embrace, understand and heal the rich complexity that makes each of us who we are. Each family has its own unique energy field, a blend of the different lineages from each parent. Sometimes there is a coherent field of confidence, vitality and creativity. But often energies of depression, anxiety, fear, greed, anger or envy, to name but a few of the negative energetic states, permeate the energy field of the family adding layers of complexity to whom each individual might be. As a result of karmic influences, one child might be more impacted by or susceptible to one energy over another. Often families designate a black sheep onto whom all the shadow aspects of the family are projected just as another is anointed to be the superstar or the savior of the family. The energy behind these designations can splatter the child's energy field and seep deeply into the core of the psyche, reducing aspects of a very complex being to a one-dimensional form. The traumas, legacies, hopes and failures coupled with the taught beliefs and accompanying stories create a cognitive and energetic culture that encompasses the individuals in the family. If the energies and beliefs of the family culture are dominant, the true essence of the individuals in the family can be subsumed under the weight of the ancestral imprints. For instance, a person, by nature, might be a very generous and kind person, but is born into a family where money and power are what is valued. If one wants to be part of the family, her kind, generous nature may be repressed and hidden until that part is seen and valued by another.

In order to fully maximize our gifts, our purpose in life and the true essence of our heart, we must identify those energies and beliefs that we carry which are not our own, heal, transform and release them so that we can claim the true essence of who we are and why we are on the planet at this time. Simultaneously, we must recognize those gifts and the positive attributes that enhance the basic essence of who we are. It is commonly believed in some circles that we choose the families to whom we are born. Often our families are well known to us and we have agreed to take on certain life lessons with one another. Sometimes these lessons are painful and challenging; other times they help us to manifest our path, such as a great musician being born into a musical family. Most commonly our early environment provides us with the fertile ground to heal that which we came into this lifetime to heal and that which we came to manifest.

Chapter 5

Claiming Our Gifts

Genevieve is a gifted and talented singer. Her mother found her voice well suited for church solos and other appropriate community venues. Genevieve aspired to be a professional singer, but her mother found this to be an unseemly profession. After bouts of severe vertigo, Genevieve sought healing work. She discovered that when she claimed her dream to be a professional singer and shed the recriminations, both energetically and verbally of her mother, her vertigo disappeared. The tension between her dreams and the desires and pronouncements of her mother had left Genevieve off balance to the extent that she could scarcely be upright. By coming into balance with her gifts, talents and path, Genevieve was in balance within herself; the physical manifestation of the imbalance healed.

One could argue that Genevieve simply should have ignored her mother from the beginning and followed her dream. Those of us who have had parents that had definite views as to which careers were acceptable and which were not understand that there is nothing simple about going against one's parents. Some parents unwittingly impart their expectations for their children's lives at a very early age, deeply embedding them in both the psyche structures of the mind and in the various layers of the energy body. Genevieve was raised in a Christian family in which using one's gift for God was an offering, but to use this gift for one's own pleasure and fame was a defilement. Although Genevieve did not *believe* that being a professional singer defiled God, she *felt* as if she were a bad person if she chose this path. What she believed in her heart and what she felt were at odds as the energy around her mother's beliefs was so strong. Genevieve had been raised in a family that had strong principles and values. These beliefs were held within the energetic frame of the family, and were supported and maintained by their church community. Genevieve believed that to go against her mother's wishes meant that she would create a tear in the energetic fabric that held the family together. This was something that she had not wanted to do.

Once Genevieve claimed her dream and stood outside of the field of her family, she began to allow more and more of herself to emerge. Although the transformation took several months, by the end of the metamorphosis Genevieve felt alive and literally sparkled with her luminous energy. Her mother did not like her decision, but was able to see and appreciate the radiance in Genevieve and slowly began to accept her decision. The relationship between them has become more honest and vibrant than ever before as Genevieve is happy and able to connect with her mother from her own core essence, rather than the conflicted place of either denying herself or defying her mother.

Through shamanic journeys, Genevieve met her spirit guides and power animals that escorted her to a deeper way of knowing and seeing what it is that she came here to do, to define her own life's purpose. Once she believed that she not only had the right but also the obligation to herself to accomplish what she came here to do, we removed via energy work the rigid and judgmental vibrations of her energy field that left her feeling like an immoral and impious woman if she pursued her path to be a successful stage actress. A healing was done for the talented part of her that had been put in a small box, hidden from her, so that the full power of her gifts could manifest.

Each of us comes into the world with our own unique gifts and talents. Many of these gifts have a genetic and energetic base to them, while others arise as a gift from spirit. The extent to which our gifts and talents are honored and developed depend on many factors. Do we live in a country and time period where our particular gifts have a venue for expression? If Michael Jordan had lived in the early 1800s, his athleticism would have benefitted his slave owner, but we would not have known of him or been able to see him fly through the air to dunk a basket from mid-court. A person's psychic and healing abilities might be greatly valued in one culture; whereas in another these gifts would be underdeveloped, in another seen as madness, and possibly the reason for persecution and a death sentence. One might be academically brilliant, but be born into a family that neither values nor has the means to foster and develop this brilliance.

Most of you who are reading this book have had the opportunity to develop your gifts and talents, but often there are factors that block the full manifestation of these gifts. Sometimes we are unaware of our talents as they were not seen or acknowledged as a child. A young boy that is gifted in playing the piano may never develop this talent if he is not exposed to a piano. This is especially true if he grows up in a family that feels piano playing is for girls and disparages boys who display this gift. Wanting to fit in, he may never be aware of this special talent. I grew up longing to play the drums, but was told repeatedly that girls do not play drums. One brave girl two years ahead of me in school broke this taboo and played the drums in the school band; she was constantly teased and ridiculed for this. She served as a stark reminder of what might happen to me if I pursued this interest.

Verbal and Energetic Messages

Often there are messages, either verbal, energetic or a mixture of the two, that convey who we are expected to be, what talents we are to develop and what interests are all right to pursue and which are not. Often when I do a soul retrieval, I find a gifted part of the self that has been lost or pushed aside. The energy field of the child absorbed, over time, the energetic thrust behind the words and messages as to who she must be. Gradually the valued parts of her are driven away as the energy of who her family wants her to be occupies the place of the gifted part.

Sometimes this part decides that it is too painful to be ignored and her passion unexpressed, and leaves to find a sacred place where this part is nurtured and guided by a wise teacher on the spiritual plane. Occasionally it leaves sensing that it will be destroyed if it stays. We might identify this exiled part by bringing back to memory the fantasies of our childhood. Often the part does not go far, lingering as a shadow, trailing behind, safely protected from harm, sending glimpses of who one could be, all the time hoping for an opening or space within the energy field in order to return. Even years later these special and gifted parts are sometimes blocked from return by the thought forms and energies that carry the message of what we are to do or who we are to be; blocking the space in the field for the part to return.

These lost or pushed-out parts can be healed, transformed and brought back by a shamanic extraction and soul retrieval. When I did an extraction for Genevieve, with the help of both my guides and hers, I gently gathered up the energies in her field that belonged to her parents and her church community and removed these energies from her field. I then did a healing for these energies and sent them back to her family and to the church bringing love and life to the rigid repressed views. In Genevieve's case, the talented part of her had not gone away, but was buried deep behind her fourth and fifth chakras. I unburied this part and brought her out for a healing which was lovingly done by one of her guides and one of mine. I watched as she expanded into her full essence after years of being repressed and pushed deep within her heart and throat. This part happily returned to Genevieve's energy body and filled up the space that had been occupied by the energy of limitation and repression from her family and church community.

Genevieve has gone on to have a successful career as a performer.

Sometimes the messages that we receive as to who we are to

be are not direct but subtle. "You are just like your father, maybe you will be a banker just like him." Because you love and admire your father, you are happy to be thought to be like him and thus you follow in the prescribed path even though you have no real desire to be a banker. Uncle Joe was a musician who traveled and lived on the road, playing in one local bar after another and was perceived as the irresponsible bum in the family. The inclination to be a musician was pushed aside after years of disparaging remarks about Uncle Joe.

Occasionally there are mixed messages within the family. The verbal message may be to have an economically secure career, but the energetics may read differently. A parent may convey one message while the energy behind it is in direct contradiction. My father wanted to be a journalist. He was in college during the Great Depression. His parents demanded that he return home to help with the family business after just two years of college. Although he was successful in the business, this was not his passion nor what he wanted to be doing. As a child, I could feel his depression as a result of being forced into a career that he did not want. He released my brother from any sense of obligation to be in the family business as he wanted him to pursue his dreams, but would jokingly voice that I should marry someone who would take over the business. He stressed, however, that I should become a certified teacher in order to have a career to fall back upon in the event of any unforeseen circumstances. The message was that my brother could dream big and that I needed to dream small, safe and practical. Although the verbal message was clear, the sense of sadness and loss that I perceived my father to have as a result of what he felt compelled to do was much stronger. I did not want to be trapped in a life that was not my choosing. Against my parents' ardent protests, I did not become a teacher, rather a political science major and upon graduation from college I joined the Peace Corps. This sent me to the village in Borneo where I would meet my teacher and onto the path of what I came here to do. In this instance I did not listen to the verbal message but honored the power of the energy that conveyed how unfulfilled my father felt. My brother followed my parents' wishes to dream big. He received an MBA, and was successful in business and banking. He lived his life energetically as my parents had, choosing the responsible path. Before he left an unfulfilling, but financially rewarding job for one that he enjoys, he revealed that he envied me as I had taken the risk to choose a career that I love and find so satisfying.

Often we are encouraged to pursue safe, productive careers and assign our creative passions to the category of hobbies. A strong resonance rang out within me when I heard Susan Orlean speak on the NPR radio program, *An Alternative Life*. After she had published seven successful books, Ms. Orlean was honored to have her life portrayed by Merle Streep in a major motion picture. In spite of success that many only dream of, her father cajoled her to go to law school, "just in case this writing thing does not work out". I have worked with a number of aspiring and actualized artists, actors, musicians and writers. In addition to raw talent, the key to being successful is to believe that you can be. Often this involves unburdening the psyche and energy field of all of the messages that conveyed this is not the correct path. Many talented high school art students are steered towards becoming a graphic designer, draftsman, or architect rather than a fine artist as these careers are deemed safer and more profitable. Aspiring musicians, writers, and actors are often encouraged to teach their craft, "just in case the dream of the big stage does not work out". Often people bargain with themselves and take the safe career path, promising themselves that they will pursue their dreams after they save a little money. Often life and family responsibilities take over and years later they look back and wonder what might have been had they followed their dream. I have worked with many people in their 40s, 50s and 60s that have had the courage to go back and reclaim the talent and gifts which they set aside.

Defining Your Path

For a number of years I have taught a ten-month biweekly workshop designed to explore and define what one's path is in this lifetime. As stated before, I believe that we all come into life with something to heal from past incarnations and with what we are to manifest in this lifetime. Since we in the West live in a very linear materialistic society, we are not often encouraged to think outside of the box or to consider what it is that we really want to do or, more specifically, what we came here to do. We are in a time of enormous transformation on the planet. It seems that we have chosen to be here at this exciting and tumultuous time in order to bring forth our wisdom and talents. Given that the global consciousness allows us to connect with the far reaches of the world, part of our work is to bring forth the deep wisdom from our previous incarnations that will help us individually, as well as collectively, to manifest the transformation that we want.

In the classes that I teach, we use shamanic journeying to meet and work with our spirit guides and power animals that, in turn, accompany and guide us in the manifestation of our path. Often one of our spirit guides hails from a previous lifetime and is with us to bring to consciousness the wisdom from that life into this one. Through the process of shamanic journeying, participants explore and connect with the internal wisdom that has been within them all along. If only, however, it was as easy as getting in touch with what we came here to do. Through journey work and consultation with our guides and power animals, we come to understand the blocks that prevent us from fully actualizing our path. There are layers of stacked voices in our heads that broadcast, often quite loudly, "This is what I should be doing with my life," and drown out the inner wisdom of what we came here to do. Once we unravel the web of energies and thought forms that have kept us from our true voice and heart, we explore ways to heal and transform these blocks. Within the safety of a collective setting, members of the group support and encourage each other in pursing their dreams, sometimes offering concrete help in the starting of a new business or creative venture. They also call each other out on the myriad excuses that are easily concocted to stay stuck.

One of the most powerful journeys that we do in the class is to explore the gifts and talents that each has received from her ancestors. Often if one has had a challenging or difficult relationship with her family, she may block from awareness the gifts that she received from them. While on a shamanic journey, I was surprised to discover that my psychic abilities came from my maternal lineage. There had been great fear and concern about my interests in developing this gift, but I later learned that it was because of their awareness of this realm that they feared it in me. Surprisingly, at the age of 97, my mother said, "If I were younger, I would be interested in learning how to do what you do." This curiosity at her age confirmed my belief that it is never too late to remember who one really is and to let go of previously held beliefs that hold one back.

While journeying to discover one's ancestral gifts, it was common to find ancestors that one had never known, but who carried a gift or talent that they had within them, a gift that may not have been nurtured by their immediate family, but was still part of the lineage. Sometimes a relative, who had been shunned or thought of poorly, carried a link to this talent, making it challenging to fully own the gift for fear of similar treatment. Others discovered that, unconsciously, they had shied away from developing a particular gift, fearing that they would not be as accomplished as someone else in the family; often, in fact, being told that this was the case. "You will never be as great of a teacher as your aunt was." Sometimes there were subtle messages not to be more successful than one's parents for fear of shaming them. Thus there was no point to pursue the path that had been seeded before birth. It was often necessary to do healing work to unravel both the cognitive and energetic base that blocked one's gift.

Releasing Negative Thought Forms and Energies from Our Field

Throughout history, there have been subtle or not so subtle messages as to who we are to be and what path is an acceptable one. This is particularly true in stratified class societies. Boys were often told that it is important to be a good provider, to be as successful as possible, that one's worth as a man will be measured by the amount of wealth that is accumulated. Even if one is not told this by the family, it is certainly a strong message that seeps into one's consciousness from the dominant culture. The millennials appear to have pushed aside this message in favor of one that encourages creativity and personal fulfillment, but they are bucking an expectation that is centuries old. Perhaps they will fall into line as did the hippies and antiwar protestors of the baby boomer era when they reached their late thirties.

Those who survived the hardships and sacrifice of the Great Depression and World War II wanted nothing more than to feel safe; it seems that many equated safety with financial security. Women called into the male-dominated workforce during the war discovered, for the most part, that they liked the freedom, sense of accomplishment and pride in doing work which, heretofore, they would not have considered nor was available to them. Just as abruptly at the war's end, they were pushed out of these jobs and told to retreat into their domestic box. Daughters of these obedient women were often advised to marry someone who would be a good provider, and that if one did have a career that it should be one that was secondary to one's responsibilities to family. Yet the underlying energetic message that was absorbed by many of these baby boomer daughters was the lack of fulfillment in their mothers' lives. This understanding comes not only from my personal experience, but also from the countless accounts from psychotherapy clients who had experienced a similar appraisal of their mothers' experience. In the seventies the women's liberation movement erupted onto the scene spawning feminist consciousness-raising groups. A common theme was the felt sense of their mothers' unhappiness and lack of gratification in their roles coupled with a yearning to be free from a narrow definition of one's path and purpose in life.

Cultural messages of who we should be may not be as energetically charged as the messages that come from one's family and immediate community, but they do have a significant impact as is exemplified by women walking away from their jobs after World War II without protest. When the family, community and cultural messages are one and the same, it is indeed challenging to override them. It can literally kill the heart and soul of one's true dreams. These pronouncements, however, are merely that and are not fact. Throughout history roles for both men and women have changed and evolved, sometimes in the direction of more freedom and in other instances with more repression. The only true compass is the light that arises in one's heart and mind that illuminates one's true purpose for being here.

A man in his early 40s came to see me. He had just been diagnosed with stage four cancer. Jack was a successful businessman, married with three children. His father had been an extremely successful businessman in New York City. Jack grew up in one of the wealthy bedroom communities of southern Connecticut from which the message of who he was to be was re-enforced from both the community and his family. Jack had rebelled to some extent in high school, had set limits on his father's abusive energy and words, but basically resided within the energetic and cultural bubble of who he was supposed to be. While in college he majored in philosophy and reported that many of his most meaningful conversations to date had been with his professors. Instead of pursuing this interest in graduate school as he longed to do, he did what he felt that he *had* to do and went into the business world.

During the healing work for Jack, I began to remove the ancestral imprint of his father's energy that embodied and carried with it all of the messages about who Jack was to be, as well as the anger, disappointment and harsh criticism that accompanied these messages. Apparently Jack's father had expected him to become a clone of himself and have his briefcase in hand by middle school. As I struggled to extract this deeply entrenched energy, Jack cried out that there was a face staring at him that terrified him. I asked if it was the face of his father. After a deep sigh, he said yes. I asked if I could remove his father's energy, he said yes as his body began to tremble with the release of the energetic burden that he had been carrying. In the soul retrieval, I found spirit guides and power animals for Jack, and a wounded part of him as a boy. There was also a bright, curious, spiritual and philosophical part of Jack that had been pushed out by his father's energy. This part trailed along outside of Jack's energy field, a trace reminder of who Jack was to be on the soul level, unable to find an opening in Jack's field to make its way back inside.

A part that was very dark and skeletal displayed the cancerous tumors as dark masses within the body. My guides told me that this part had carried his father's energy, and without this energy, it was but a skeleton. The energy had been so toxic that it had resulted in a life-threatening illness. I worked as hard as I could to channel divine light from my healing guides to transform and heal the cancerous tumors. Finally my guides told me to take this part into my being and heal it from within my own energy field. I did this and held this part of Jack within until I saw light and form return to the being of this part. While I was doing this, my guides were busy healing the father's energy that had been removed. The father had already crossed over but his holographic vibration was in the room as he had come to be part of the healing, to collect the healed energy that he had left behind and to be a support to Jack in any way that he could. Jack's father did not want his son to carry his dark, angry energy, and was relieved and grateful that it had been removed. He told me to tell Jack that he was there for him as a guide if he wanted him to be, and asked his forgiveness for all that he had done to harm him from the ignorance of his personality in this lifetime. By doing a healing for Jack's father, we released both Jack and his father from this angry driven, controlling energy. Jack's father will no longer need to carry this energy into his next lifetime, allowing him to begin a new life unburdened by this angry controlling energy.

At Jack's next CAT scan, the doctors were delighted to find that the cancerous cells in the major tumor were in the dying process and that no new cancerous cells were revealed. I do not believe that the shamanic work alone helped to reverse the growth of Jack's cancer. I do believe, however, that the removal of the toxic energies that were within Jack's energy field combined with the return of healed parts and parts that represented the true essence of who Jack is enabled him to utilize the cancer treatments. I do not suggest that shamanism is a replacement for cancer treatment, but as a way to return the soul and the psyche to wholeness so that the body can begin its own healing process, freed from toxic and unwanted energies.

This is a dramatic, albeit, true account of the degree to which we can absorb the messages and negative energies about who we are to be that override the true essence of who we are. The extremes that the wiser aspects of our soul essence go to challenge us to awaken and to heal is indeed impressive. These energies do not always make us sick physically. Sometimes we become depressed as my father did; others shut down, numbing themselves through mindless activities or addictive behaviors, being only half present to their lives. It is important to realize that it is not selfish to do what we came here to do, despite the protests of those who think otherwise, but it is essential for our overall well-being and the well-being of all. Marianne Williamson's poem,[10] *Our Deepest Fear*, which was incorporated into Nelson Mandela's inauguration address in 1994, stated:

Our deepest fear is not that we are inadequate. Our deepest fear is that we are powerful beyond measure. Who am I to be brilliant, gorgeous, talented, fabulous? Actually, who Are you not to be? You are a child of God. Your playing small does not serve the world. There is nothing enlightened about shrinking so that other people won't feel insecure around you. We are meant to shine, as children do. We were born to make manifest the glory of God that is within us. It's not just in some of us, it's in everyone. And as we let our own light shine, we unconsciously give other people permission to do the same. As we are liberated from our fear, our presence automatically liberates others.

Before we face and begin to heal negative energies that burden us and hold us back from our true essence, take a moment to recognize and claim the many gifts that we brought into this incarnation. Some of these gifts are part of our true essence; part of who we have always been. Other gifts are an accumulation of skills and abilities that we have amassed in our previous lifetimes. Some are the genetically and energetically inherited gifts from our ancestors. Regardless from where they stem, it is important that we recognize, honor and develop them. Make some time to meditate or journey; ask that a gift or talent that you have not brought forward rise to consciousness. If you would take ten minutes each day to see what might surface, you might be surprised to see what is buried within. As we claim more of who we are and honor and embrace the gifts that our ancestors and our karmic history have bestowed upon us, we lay the groundwork to stand fully in our power and joy. In doing this, we break the shackles of the cognitive and energetic burdens that we have conveyed for our ancestors, freeing them as well as ourselves.

Chapter 6

Releasing Our Ancestral Burdens

Like an invisible veil, we pass the energetic imprint from one generation to the next. Sometimes it is light, a faint reminder from whence we came. Other times it is feels like a well-worn cloak weighting us down, slowing our pace, tiring us out. For some it is worn like a noose around the neck, suffocating and strangling the life force out of our very being.

The energies that we carry from our ancestors are varied, felt and experienced in differing ways. Our ancestry is not a monolithic entity, but is comprised from both of our parents' families, our grandparents' families and their grandparents' families, and on and on. Many take advantage of the numerous companies that trace one's ancestral lineage through DNA testing. Our genetic ancestry is but a small part of what we absorb from our predecessors. Each new family unit creates its own unique blend of ancestral energies. Some of these energies are so robust that they dominate the combined field and, like a rolling stone, gather momentum from one generation to the next often overpowering their partners' own energetic contributions. Often people choose partners that have a familiar *feel* to them, a similar energetic imprint. This energetic imprint often overrides racial, class or cultural considerations as the familiarity of the energy, for good or for ill, can be compelling. There is a strong unconscious pull to find someone with whom we can either heal the wounds from our families, but all too often, given the divorce rate, choose someone with whom to reenact them.

These reenactments are not limited to romantic partners, but are played out between various family configurations, friends and within the workplace. The cornerstone of most psychological theories and practice centers on examining, understanding and healing the myriad dynamics that arise within the family unit that cause pain and stunt growth. What is missing is an understanding and awareness of how the energetic undercurrents pervade and shape the cognitive awareness of the healing process. Although the energetic imprints are part of and contribute to the felt experience of our interactions, they are not the same. The energetic imprints shape how we experience reality and how we are drawn to certain encounters and behaviors that our rational mind would readily block if the power of the energetics were not so strong.

Through an opportunity to work with an adult daughter and her mother, I was able to see and experience directly how the energetic wounds are passed from one generation to the next. When I first began to work with the daughter, Jesse was a bright, beautiful, talented and personable woman in her late 30s. She was married with one daughter. Initially she was depressed, very fragile and prone to viewing herself as less than others, unable to handle only the basic tasks of living. Jesse was the fourth child of a clinically depressed mother who spent much of Jesse's early life cloistered in her room with occasional hospitalizations for indeterminate periods of time as it was the era when long hospitalizations were the norm. Jesse tried to be the perfect child, asking nothing of her parents and taking care of her mother as best she could. Jesse even accompanied her father to events that ordinarily her mother would have attended, cooked dinner each night, cleaned and assumed many of the domestic duties of the household. Jesse is a talented dancer and was invited to be part of the Boston Ballet School. Her parents nixed this opportunity as her father worked and her mother was unable to drive her there. It did not occur to anyone in the family to find alternate transportation or find a ballet school closer to home so Jesse could continue her studies; thus the one thing that fed her soul was taken away.

Towards the end of her years in high school, Jesse's facade

of competence and grace began to crumble. She told her parents that she was struggling to cope, but they were unable to hear her pleas for help, needing to see her as the competent caretaker that she had been. They needed her to run the household and keep everything functioning. After a manic episode, Jesse was hospitalized for severe depression. Once she recovered, Jesse then struggled to put herself through college with no financial or emotional support from her parents. Another hospitalization ensued. Mired in a deep depression after a lifetime of being who she thought that she needed to be for her mother's survival, Jesse had no idea who she was or what she felt, let alone appreciate and embrace her beauty and talents. Much of the essence of whom she was had been literally sucked out of her, replaced by the depressed energy field of her mother. After several years of traditional psychotherapy, group therapy and shamanic extraction and soul retrieval work, Jesse began to reclaim herself. She found her voice, studied ballet again and became a gifted potter. As Jesse began to feel better and experienced the positive effects of the shamanic work, she asked if I would do a soul retrieval for her mother.

Jesse's mother was also a beautiful, talented, bright and personable woman, in her 70s, who had endured years of psychotherapy and shock treatments. Mary even received shock treatments when she was pregnant with Jesse, assured that the baby would in no way be affected. From a shamanic and energetic perspective, a baby is significantly impacted by shock treatments. Mary had grown up in a large family with a mother who was also severely depressed and had died when Mary was 13. She also was expected to take care of the family as Jesse had been. Whenever she stepped aside from these expectations, trying to claim herself, the recriminations and guilt were swift and debilitating. Her memories of her childhood were scant as she experienced herself as an invisible shell. Mary was exceptionally bright and attractive, attended a good college and was successful there, which was a feat for a woman of her generation. She had wanted to be an airplane stewardess, a plum job at the time, but by her senior year, her depression was quite severe, her sense of self extremely fragile. In an attempt to find some form of container, she married and began to have children, her depression at times debilitating.

Both mother and daughter, and most likely Mary's mother as well, lived in a web of invisibility and disconnection. Neither had been seen by their family beyond what they could do to make their family's lives more comfortable; neither had a sense of who they really were. Mary told me that Jesse had been the perfect child; she did not think that she would have survived without her love and care. When I raised Jesse's own struggles with depression, she looked puzzled, then allowed that perhaps Jesse had a rough year or two, but clearly she had not let in the level of Jesse's pain, seeing her as her perfect child and caretaker, rendering the true Jesse invisible just as Mary had been.

Both responded well to shamanic work and were able to release the invisibility cloaks that they had worn their entire lives and welcome back key parts of their soul. The sense of being unseen, unknown, unsupported appeared to be the dominant ancestral imprint that was in need of healing. The power of this energetic imprint was strong enough to alter their biochemistry resulting in major depression. A major cause of depression is the loss of key parts of oneself, which was true for both Jesse and Mary. There were parts of both of them that had faded away as they were not seen or acknowledged by anyone including themselves. Each had unwittingly given part of her energy to her respective mother in hopes that her mother might have enough energy to give something back. When Jesse gave part of her energy to her mother, the void left by this gift was filled with Mary's depressed energy laying the foundation for her own depression. When I removed Mary's energy from Jesse's field, a healing was done for this energy by my guides who returned it to Mary. As Mary's healed energy was blown into her crown chakra, my guides pulled Jesse's energy out of Mary's field. A healing was then done for Jesse's energy before it was returned to her. Mary benefitted from Jesse's soul retrieval as she felt more enlivened after Jesse's healing; this paved the way for her own soul retrieval.

The most challenging aspect of the work was to facilitate the awareness that they carried the *same* ancestral imprint of feeling invisible to those in the family. They both believed that they were only seen and valued for their role as caretaker. Irrespective of how others in the family perceived them and their role, this is how each felt and was the cognitive and energetic reality in which each lived. All too often people tell another that how they feel is wrong, not accurate, without fully grasping that each of us lives within our own energetic and cognitive field that is unique to us. We each have a perspective on what is true, what our reality is that differs slightly from another.

Mary had difficulty fully absorbing how wounded Jesse had been by her depression and her inability to truly be a mother to Jesse. It was too painful to see that Jesse had suffered as she had. Jesse still longed for a mother who could see and hear her past pain and acknowledge her suffering. She had difficulty letting go of the hurt and anger that her mother could not yet do this. Both saw the other flower and come more into their own. Thus Mary saw Jesse as doing fine, so there was no need to dwell on or go into the past. Jesse had glimpses of who her mother was becoming and longed for her to be the mother that she had never had, but first she needed her mother to recognize the harm her depression had caused her. The difficulty that they both had in acknowledging their shared journey lessened their ability to connect on the deep level for which each so longed. As each more fully healed and began to own the bright beautiful beings that they are, their ability to fully see each other emerged.

I believe that a major part of the difficulty in their initial inability to see their shared pain and shared imprint arose from the societal imprint of assessing blame and responsibility for a person's woundedness. The deeply entrenched cultural belief that if something is wrong, someone is to blame. It was hard for Mary to listen to Jesse's pain as she feared being blamed for all of Jesse's problems. The fear of being blamed often blinds us to the fullness and complexity of our experiences as we strive to bury our misdeeds, denying that they are there. From my professional experience, the fear of being blamed or judged thwarts one's ability to heal as culturally there is shame in being wrong, thus we avoid it at all cost. Many do not grasp that we all make mistakes. In each lifetime our soul wants to grow and expand. If we allow ourselves to learn from our errors, then we foster our soul's development. If we do not judge ourselves, but rather attempt to understand our actions, we will grow and thrive.

Conversely, Jesse had difficulty releasing her hurt and disappointment with her mother as it was a deep wound that she longed for her mother to acknowledge. The inability to forgive keeps us frozen in the pain. Although it is important to feel, understand and process our pain, hurt and anger, it is equally important not to hold onto painful memories as if they are precious nuggets. Our feelings are fluid, but if we constantly retell our stories of woe, they become rigidified thought forms, which results in remaining stuck in old patterns and painful memories, forcing one to exist in the energy of the initial hurt. It takes a skilled therapist to discern when a client has processed her pain and hurt enough to bring it to a point where it can be released and healed. Often when I do healing work for a client, I will find a ball of resentment towards one that harmed them which is eating away aspects of their core essence, trapping them in the experience. I urge clients when the initial pain has subsided to adopt a both/and approach. One can feel all of the pain and hurt while simultaneously having compassion and understanding for the one who wounded us. In order to fully heal we must develop compassion both for ourselves and for others as we move out of the dualistic thinking of the dominant culture to see the rich complexities of who we are.

The Compassionate Heart

If I could wave a magic wand and extract a debilitating tendency from within our culture, it would be the tendency to blame and judge, rather than to understand. For years politicians in the United States set the tone by seeking to blame and find fault with those with whom they disagreed rather than to seek common ground; to admit a mistake was a sign of weakness. President Obama's ability to take responsibility when he made a mistake and to walk us through the complexity of issues rather than speaking in sound bites was initially refreshing. The media attacked him for his lack of a clear message and for sounding too professorial. Soon he, as well, was forced to speak simply so his words could be turned into sound bites. The media did not seem to have the capacity to digest and report the complexity of an issue and yearned for a clear message that could easily be picked apart. We are fundamentally a culture that thinks in the dichotomies of right and wrong, black and white. It seems easier to claim that someone did harm and hold onto anger and hurt than it is to consider the factors that went into causing them to act in a harmful way. I am in no way advocating that people cease to be held responsible for their actions. What I am saying is that if we did not first blame ourselves or the other person for hurtful actions, but instead tried compassionately to understand why either we or the other person acted as they did, people would be more likely to take responsibility for their actions, the fear of blame and self-recrimination lessened.

When Mary, without self-blame, takes in that her depression and sense of being invisible caused her to see and treat her children as if they were also invisible, then she will be more present to Jesse and her other children around their pain. When

Jesse feels more compassion and understanding for what her mother had gone through, then it will be easier for her mother to see how Jesse has been harmed. No one goes into parenthood planning to do harm to their children; thus when this happens, as it always does to some extent, it is often too painful to face. As a culture, we do not carry the capacity to see how difficult it is to be human. We expect perfection and are disappointed when we do not deliver it or receive it.

A key ingredient in our ability to heal is to develop a compassionate heart towards ourselves and others. Each time we make a mistake or act in ways that we wish we had not, we can instead pause, take a deep breath and see this as a teaching moment, a time to learn and to heal. Gently ask ourselves what just happened that we acted in the way that we did. Did this action come from our true heart or were we feeling threatened in some way and responded from this threat? What are we to learn from this situation, what is the teaching? Did this reaction come from deep within or did the response arise from an ancestral imprint, as we behaved as a parent did under a similar situation? I shudder when I look back over my life at some of the things that I did and said, or when I behaved in a way other than how I wished I had. I have a choice as to whether I hold onto my misconduct in a shamed-based manner, whether I create stories to justify my poor actions based on how wronged I was or whether I see the lessons and teachings in these incidents and affirm and take in how much I have grown and changed over the years. It is only through our compassion for our life journey that we will find the courage to confront and heal the demons from our past.

Unraveling the Ancestral Imprints

We come into this world as a pure soul essence that carries an overlay of our prior incarnations. At the core of who we are is pure love and a direct connection to the divine. We have the capacity to be one with all that is. We often lose connection to our core essence through the layers of cultural, racial, spiritual and familial imprints. A meditation practice or some form of spiritual practice is extremely helpful as it is through meditation and prayer that we strengthen the core of who we are and hasten the unraveling of these imprints. Once we identify imprints that are not useful, we can dissolve them through prayer and meditation, by sitting with them and then releasing them from our energy field. The mind holds them in place and the mind can release them.

We amass these imprints in a variety of ways. As with Jesse and her mother, Mary, the imprint of invisibility was absorbed from one to the other. It came in by osmosis. Mary felt unseen and existed as a shadow of who she really was as her mother before her had. What we absorb into our field is reflected out; often we respond to others as we were responded to. Because Mary felt so unseen and the energy around this so strong, it was hard for her to see those around her or to believe that she mattered or would have any impact on another. Jesse absorbed this imprint of invisibility, and assumed and experienced that she was not seen by others. In social situations she felt petrified and did not know what to say. As she stood frozen and still, her sense of invisibility became more entrenched. Jesse's role within the family had been as caretaker, thus she took excellent care of her husband and daughter while ignoring the needs that she did not know she had.

Many take on ancestral imprints through soul loss. If a parent is violent and angry toward her small child, part of the child's soul essence will pop out and in its place the angry energy of the parent will occupy the space where the part of the child's soul essence was. This angry energy sits in the energy field like a bomb waiting to be detonated by a similar angry outburst that was the root cause of the soul loss. The child grows up fearing angry outbursts as these outbursts activate the rage within his own field, a rage that is not his but that of his mother. The child experiences both the assault hurling towards him as well as the activation of the rage within resulting in a terrifying explosion of effect. One person told me that he was unaware of feelings of anger until he heard his disembodied voice screaming. Once triggered by another's anger or disapproval, he began to yell to ward off the attack that he feared was coming, sending it back from whence it came like a boomerang.

In Jack's case, a core part of his essence retreated deep within himself and left behind a protective part that arose like a defensive mechanism designed to keep him safe. This protective part contained his father's angry energy and took on the irate judgmental voice of his father. Its job was to be powerful enough to match his father's energy. Although Jack is a gentle soul, he reported having difficulty with his anger toward his wife and children. His father's angry voice and energy would flow out of him in situations that were similar to those in which his father had been abusive to him. His father often went on a rampage when toys were strewn everywhere and not picked up upon first request. Like clockwork, when Jack's children did not pick up their toys when first asked, his father's anger would spew out of him. Afterward Jack would be filled with shame and remorse for behaving just as his father had.

Sometimes an ancestral imprint flows in through energy cords. The depressive or anxious energy of the mother can flow through the placenta into the growing baby and be absorbed into the being of the unborn child. This can also happen after we are born. In a soul retrieval that I did for Joyce, I saw her as a small child lying on the bed next to her mother sending her pure heart energy into her mother through a beautiful stream of light flowing from her heart chakra. As the mother filled with her light, she sent back the gray painful energy of loss and abandonment as Joyce's father had left them. The energy of loss occupied the space in her field where her beautiful light energy had been and was centered around and within her heart chakra haunting her with pain throughout her life. Each time that Joyce was with someone in great pain, she unconsciously sent her loving energy to the other and received their pain into her body through the pathways that had been established with her mother. After several years the painful energy she had absorbed was more prevalent than her loving heart energy; Joyce had given away too much of herself. Joyce became anorexic around the age of 11 and continued to struggle throughout her adolescence. She had absorbed so much pain from others while unwittingly surrendering part of herself that she did not have the energy to fight for herself. Because the source of her distress had an energetic component, it was difficult to fully unravel psychologically the source of her pain. It is important to note that one can channel loving healing energy from the divine frequency realm through the crown of the head and out through the heart chakra without harming oneself or surrendering any of one's own energy.

It is quite common to find that a person can absorb ancestral imprints from a combination of factors. It can occur through the absorption of an imprint by osmosis, through the giving away of our energy through an energy cord, and in turn receiving the energy of the one to whom we gave the energy, or through part of us leaving and another's energy popping in to fill the void left behind. Often one factor is primary but sometimes all three ways of taking on an imprint is present within one person. A key to healing these imprints is to understand that this energy is not part of our core essence but for good or ill it is part of our inheritance. We do not need to carry it. It is a gift to our ancestors to heal and release these imprints as they are freed when we are freed. By healing ourselves we have the potential to heal all who came before and all who will come after.

After many years of working as a psychotherapist, I could sense and feel that there is much more to our emotional and physical distress than what we can process and discover through talk therapy. When I returned to Malaysian Borneo to study with the teacher who taught me the secrets and power of ancient healing practices, practices that put the energetic aspect of our being at the center of health and well-being, I began to comprehend the power of the energetic realms to shape who we are. But we are more than just our energetic being. Our thoughts and beliefs play a central role in drawing energy to us and in turning fluid energetic states into concrete ones through a constant retelling of our life narrative.

Chapter 7

Walking Through the Land Mines of Projection

There is a famous scene in the Tom Cruise movie, Mission: Impossible, *in which he is to steal a sacred object. He is lowered on wires from the ceiling and then has to make his way through layers and layers of infrared lines of alarms that exist multidimensionally. We watch amazed as he magically makes his way through this potential death trap, knowing exactly where to step until he grasps what he came to claim. When I think of this scene, I think of how many of us walk through life, trying not to trip the alarms that set off the layers of projections that we carry. Some of these projections have been plastered to our field by others, while some are created within us to be hurled out as protection for our wounded parts. As long as we stay small and obedient, we will not activate these layers of projections and, hopefully, we will be safe.*

Projection is a psychological term that describes the process by which one ascribes unowned or split-off parts of oneself onto another. A person that is overweight will comment negatively on every fat person that he sees, disparaging them for their size, unable to come to terms with his own self-hate at being overweight. A person who is feeling angry, but is afraid to acknowledge this to herself, let alone her partner, may accuse her partner of being angry at her, provoking a confrontation so that her anger can be released. This is often done without any conscious awareness of what is happening. For the projection to be taken in by the other, it needs to resonate with him, which in psychological terminology is called an introjection. If a Rhodes Scholar is called stupid, she will undoubtedly shrug this comment off as the other person's problem. A brilliant child, a potential Rhodes Scholar, repeatedly called stupid by a father that feels inferior to his son's brilliance, might take in this comment as a fact, take on the self-concept of someone who is not bright and then live within the energy and belief of this projection, never fully realizing or developing the brilliant mind that he has. If a teacher chides him for his lack of skill or motivation, he will take in this comment as true, reinforcing what he already believes about himself.

As children, we are vulnerable to the spoken and unspoken messages that we receive from our parents and teachers. A person's complex ego structure is not fully formed until around the age of twenty-five. For the first twenty-five years of our life we absorb others' projections and the next twenty-five we try to remove them so we can discover who we truly are. I have known and worked with many beautiful, bright and talented people who do not see their own beauty and gifts. These gifts are buried under the negative comments and projections of others and are held energetically in the energy field.[11]

Identifying Projections and Thought Forms

Before ancestral and karmic imprints can be healed and removed, we have to identify the projections and thought forms that hold the imprints in place. As a child, Peter's father screamed at him that he was a lazy no good bum if he did not do his homework and clean his room in a timely manner. As an adult, each time Peter is late for a project or does not have things properly organized, he hears a voice that tells him that he is a lazy no good bum. When his children are behaving as normal kids that have difficulty keeping their rooms clean and getting their homework done on their dad's time line, Peter hears his own father's voice in his head and recites the same demoralizing words that his father so often uttered to him. While we all agree that clean rooms and completed homework are good things to aspire to, it does not make one a lazy no good bum if one does not always accomplish this. Peter is more likely to yell at his kids when he is struggling to meet a deadline, his father's voice and energy awakened, driving him on. This is the nature of projections. When an uncomfortable feeling state is activated within us, it is as if a live wire has been tripped that sends old, damaging sparks to anyone within its reach.

My mother often threw large parties when I was growing up. Of course, I was expected to help. This help would vary depending on my age. Initially I was to be good, have no needs and expect nothing for the day or two leading up to the big event. Even a request for a peanut butter and jelly sandwich would be enough to trigger a torrent of rage, name calling and banishment to my room for what seemed like an eternity. As I grew older, I had age appropriate tasks such as setting the table, cleaning, and walking to the store for the inevitable forgotten necessities. Since I was a child, I never quite accomplished the tasks to my mother's standards. On the rare occasions that I did, I felt as if I had reached a state of magical grace. The energy of the days leading up to the party was filled with high anxiety. Would everything be done to perfection so that the party would be a success or would one minor thing go wrong, bringing the goal of perfection crashing down, everything ruined?

Since most of my adult friends had suffered through the party perfection preparation hell of the 1950s and 60s and worked outside of the home full-time, our parties were much more laid-back, usually potlucks, with no one caring if there were clean hand towels in the bathroom. But there were those occasions when family or others that I *assumed* expected party perfection would come to visit. I *felt* as if I had no choice but to do everything to perfection. On those occasions I would wince as I witnessed myself transform into the anxious fanatical person that my mother had been. Since I rarely ventured into party perfection hell, I would spend hours searching the recesses of my brain, trying to remember all of the things that I was to do to achieve the magical perfection. On one such occasion when I was feeling extremely frantic, my then eight-year-old son burst into tears and said that he hated who I became when I gave big parties. "You run around angry, barking orders and yelling at me." In that moment I hugged him with the realization that I was subjecting him to the same craziness that I hated as a child. Not only did I take in my mother's idea of what it meant to give the perfect party, I took on her energy and became her. After I hugged Josh and apologized, I took a deep breath and tried to calm and center myself. Clearly the perfect party depended much more on an open-hearted atmosphere with good conversation than it did on the proper place setting. Yet the energetic feeling for the need for perfection was stronger than rational thought. It felt as if I would be a failure if I did not do it just as my mother had done. On a very deep level, I had absorbed not only her beliefs but all of the energy that accompanied these beliefs down to projecting onto my son how he was to act. I expected him to behave as I had failed to by anticipating all that needed to be done to make the party a success while doing it to perfection as a mere child of eight. I was passing onto him a very silly and hurtful cultural and ancestral imprint that had nothing to do with entertaining and having a good time.

Each time I felt compelled to entertain in grand fashion or had a family gathering, I struggled to stay calm. Occasionally I found myself slipping into the frantic energy despite my best intentions. Over the years the frenetic energy lessened, yet a level of mild anxiety still persisted. If something as minor as the imprint around party preparation was challenging to change, how do we change those projections and energetic imprints that cut to the core of who we believe ourselves to be?

There are steps to take that help us to identify when our unconscious feelings or imprints are arising before we hurl them on another as a projection of our own mind. Each time we have a negative thought about another or assume that another is having a hurtful thought about us, stop and ask, "Where does this come from?" For instance, you need help with a project. You think of asking your friend, Joan, for help, but then the nattering in your head lists all of the reasons why Joan will not want to help you. As the list grows, you begin to feel angry at Joan for her unwillingness to help. Then you begin to feel sorry for yourself that you are all alone and have no one to help you with this project. As the internal rant goes on, you realize that you have worked yourself into a frenzy about something that is an odd creation of your own mind.

As soon as you can catch yourself, take a deep breath and breathe into the origin of this silliness. You have not even asked Joan for help, yet you are angry at her for saying no. Is this a familiar situation from your childhood based on the lack of support you felt as a child? Are you feeling overburdened and resentful towards others for asking you for help, and thus assume that Joan will not want to help you? Were there messages from your family about asking for and giving help to others that were negative or stimulated such a mental rant? As adults, we have a right to ask a friend for help and the friend has the right to say no if it is not something that they can do. The rational part of us knows this, but the need to ask has, in this instance, released a torrid of irrational feelings that result from unhealed negative energy and beliefs that we have either taken in from another and/or absorbed from a painful situation.

As a psychologist, I have listened to self-inflicted pain as clients torment themselves through the projection of their own fears onto another, living out their worst-case scenario before a situation arises. I have sat dumbstruck as clients have railed at me for the negative things that they *believe* me to be thinking and feeling about them when nothing can be further from the truth. Working with clients' projection is at the center of the healing process in psychotherapy. Projections are a road map to wounds and traumas. They cause us untold hours of pain and suffering when the entire drama is occurring within us rather than without. When we send a projection to another, we are continuing the negative energetic exchange.

As a shamanic practitioner, I had hoped that projections would simply be healed through the removal and transformation of the energy of the projections. In some instances this was true. But for many, the attachment to and the energetic tenacity of the negative feeling state requires further work. One needs to be able to identify that the torturous nattering of the mind is just this and not, in fact, truth.

Do Not Believe Everything You Think

Many believe all the thoughts and feelings that flow through the mind to be fact. "I am stupid and selfish." "It is wrong to say what you really believe." "The most important thing is to get ahead, even if you have to hurt someone else to do this." There can be an endless flow of chatter that swirls around in the mind that is pure poppycock. Some experience cracks in believing what their mind tells them when they encounter warring voices. Often we ask, "Which is the true voice?" In the last decade there has been a growing acceptance within the field of psychology that we have different parts and protectors to keep us safe and functioning from the demons of our past.[12] There is a part of me that tried to be the good girl and do everything that my mother wanted for the party to be perfect; this part carries a sense of failure and anxiety. There is another part that felt angry for how I was treated and thought that the whole focus on party perfection was ridiculous. Each part has a set of beliefs and feelings. We are very complex beings and carry different feelings and beliefs within the same situation. Often several aspects of who we are can be activated at once, creating confusion within us. Often it is less important to discern which voice is correct than it is to determine which voice represents our true heart, to allow our own internal wisdom to arise.

In the mid-eighties I became a student and practitioner of Vipassana meditation. One aspect of the practice is to examine the nature of mind while meditating. One is to see what thought arises, note it and let it go. If a thought persists again and again, then note it as something that needs attention or healing. As I immersed myself in this meditation practice, I was shocked and dismayed at the strange and unimportant things with which my mind was cluttered. I learned not to listen to or believe all of the strange meanderings of my mind. Through this practice, I became aware of the level to which I placed myself in the center of the universe, believing that all of the actions that those close to me took had something to do with me rather than a reflection of who they are and what is occurring in their life at the moment. Whether intended or not, my mother left me with the impression that I was responsible for her happiness and that my behavior, for good or ill, would determine her contentment in life. Thus I unconsciously assumed that others' actions held the same power to make or break my happiness, not realizing that one's joy in life arose from the peace that flows from being connected to one's inner truth and to the divine energy that is in everything if we take the time to notice. It is not dependent on what another does or does not do. As I began a shamanic practice several years later, I realized that I would not have been able to discern the teachings from my spirit guides from the ramblings of my mind if it had not been for this meditation practice.

Feelings Are Not Fact

Our feelings are extremely important and serve as a guidepost to our inner world. They tell us a great deal about ourselves and the root of our imprints and projections, but our feelings are not fact. They are energetic vibrations that flow within and around us, and only become fact when we concretize them through the constant retelling of the same hurt over and over again until it becomes a stuck energetic block in our energy field and psyche. Over the years, some of my long-term clients felt abandoned when I went on vacation. It was important to listen to and honor their feelings, but the reality was that I was not abandoning them; I was simply going away for two weeks. If I never came back or refused to see them when I did return, then this would be abandonment. So although some of my clients felt abandoned, they were not abandoned. It is important to make this distinction as we can grow our feelings into something big, even if it is not accurate. The feeling of abandonment and the pain around this is real and stems from times when one was actually abandoned. It is normal for these feelings to arise when they are triggered by a loss or sense of disconnection. However, when we project the feelings of abandonment onto a situation in which we are not being abandoned, we become engulfed in the old wound, but are unable to heal it. Blinded to what is actually occurring in the present, we lose the distance and perspective to work on and heal the old feelings of abandonment that have been triggered by a two-week separation. A skilled therapist can help a client to understand this dynamic and get to a place where real healing can occur. The goal is to be able to honor the feelings of abandonment, understand the root cause of these feelings, while cognitively understanding that feelings aside, one is not actually being abandoned. However, in one's everyday life misunderstandings occur and relationships are damaged or even ended over projections of an old wound onto a relatively minor occurrence.

As a psychotherapist working with couples, I have observed each partner hurl projections from their unhealed past onto their partner, lost behind a veil of projection, unable to see the person with whom they had fallen in love. Instead they only perceive someone whom they have loved that had harmed them in some way. We are energetically encased in imprints from our families, our society and our culture, and to the belief systems that accompany and cement the imprints into our psyche and energy fields. Suzy came from an accomplished, but critical family. She grew up feeling that she could never measure up to her family's expectation. At a certain point she gave up trying. She married Don, an all-around nice guy who lacked ambition and drive, but who also came from a successful family. Initially they were happy as they shared similar values regarding work and leisure time. Each had chosen a lifestyle based on a reaction to the pressure that they felt from their respective families. Before long a growing unease with their own choices regarding their work and lifestyle began to emerge, but, unable to see the unrest surfacing from within, they projected their growing unhappiness onto each other. Soon the negative words that each had heard as a child regarding their lack of ambition began to flow from their mouths as they bombarded each other with the painful words that haunted them as children.

Couples often come together around similar interests and similar imprints, both positive and negative ones. Each couple has a choice as to whether they will support each other as they heal their earlier wounds or whether they will reenact them. Once we recognize the imprints and thought forms as coming from another source and not who we and our partner truly are, we begin to heal and become the person we came here to be. But just as important, we begin to see the other person as who they are and not the myriad projections from our past. Suzy and Don had each developed a rebellious stance to counter the pressure that they felt from their families to succeed. It was a stance that protected them from feeling as if they were a failure; "after all, who wants all of the pressure, responsibility and materialism that come from being successful". The drawback of rebelling against one's family is that it kept each of them from realizing their own dreams and ambitions. For each to acknowledge individually that they had dreams and ambition meant that they would need to give up the rebellious protective stance that had served them well. One can feel quite vulnerable and scared at the prospect of giving up a defense that protected one from psychological attack. Thus it was safer to project their repressed desire for achievement onto their partner, be upset with the other for not being more successful, all the while suppressing that they wanted more from life than just getting by in a job in which one is not fulfilled.

The stumbling block in their relationship came when Suzy began to criticize Don for not helping with the simplest of household chores. Since Don's parents frequently referred to him as lazy, this criticism was easily taken in via what psychotherapists term as an introjection, the energy of the complaint activating not only feelings of failure, but a renewed desire to rebel; as rebellion was his defense against criticism and feelings of not being good enough. Don repeatedly forgot to take the trash out, pick his clothes up from the floor or help in any way reverting to his teenage behavior. He began to view Suzy as his nagging parents and withdrew from her, refusing to acknowledge that he expected her to do the lion's share of the housework while acting as he did in a passive aggressive manner. Increasingly Suzy felt critical of Don for not only being lazy around the house, but also for lacking ambition. Suzy, a bright and creative person, denied her own talents and dreams, unconsciously berating herself for not owning her talents by projecting these feelings onto Don. It took several sessions to unravel the various projections, unacknowledged dreams and feelings of not being good enough before they came to realize that they each wanted more out of life than working in dead-end jobs. As each began to give voice to the pressure and criticism of their youth that had thwarted an avenue to define their own journey in life, they started to see each other as the person they once loved and as one who could be an ally in finding more meaning in their lives, individually and collectively.

Each member of a couple has a choice as to whether he or she sees the other as a source of support as one goes through a life-changing transformation or as the reason that they are stuck in the situation that they are in. It takes courage to choose the former as the cognitive and energetic patterns are firmly established. For growth and healing to occur one must honor the foundation of their love and agree to be on the same side supporting one another rather than as an opponent to be defeated. By acknowledging and working both with our projections and the protective defenses that we developed to keep our young psyches intact, we can heal.

We tend to focus our time and attention on what others have done to us and how we have been harmed, but do not examine how we have imbued others with motives, deeds and harm through the lens of our imprints, putting their true essence out of focus. When I am upset with a person, I first ask myself why I am so upset with them. What part from my past has crept into the interchange that I need to look at and own as coming from energies and beliefs that I still carry? Yes, there are legitimate things that people do to us that are at best insensitive and at worst downright mean and hurtful. It is important to confront people on their bad behavior in these situations, but it is equally as important to be clear what our role is in being so upset with them.

Shame

One of the most insidious of the energetic transfers or projections is the energy of shame. When a person is raped, the feeling of shame is overwhelming, but it is not just from the fact that one's body has been violated and ravaged in the most despicable way imaginable, but also from absorbing the shameful energy of the perpetrator. Most dissociate during traumatic events. As a part of the soul essence escapes the body to avoid the full frontal attack of a violent soul-shattering event, the energy of the perpetrator floods into the vacuum that is left from this departure, rendering the victim of the abuse racked with the perpetrator's negative and shameful energy.

A father who unconsciously struggles with the shame of being a failure projects these feelings onto his children by incessantly chiding them in the most humiliating ways for not being good enough. Depending on his children's karmic imprint, one might shatter under the barrage of negativity and shame reducing one to a mere shadow of what he might become. Another might stare back at his father vowing to prove him wrong by becoming more successful than his hapless father, energetically, but silently, hurling the negative comments back at him. While another might absorb the shameful sense of failure by acting out using drugs, joining gangs or creating a life that resonates with what his father predicts he will be. In each case the underlying shameful feelings dominate the core psychic structure. Even the one who aspires to a life of success lives in terror that others will one day see the horrible person that he truly is while also grappling with feelings of being a fraud. All too often these deeply buried feelings are passed along to their progeny keeping the shameful sensation of being a failure alive from one generation to the next.

Meditation techniques assist us in becoming aware of all of the energies and beliefs that we carry that have nothing to do with who we truly are. When we are flooded with shame or have an extreme reaction to a situation, pause, take a few calming breaths and ask from whence do these feelings stem? Are there other times that they have occurred in this fashion? Do they arise from my true heart or are they energies and beliefs that I absorbed? Sit quietly and follow your breath. Do not think of the answer, but still your mind so the true answer from your heart can emerge. These energies cannot be released until they are brought to consciousness, identified as not part of who you truly are. Watch as an understanding that you no longer need to carry these energies, or listen to the ugly nattering in the mind that originated from another to torment your heart and soul, begins to float away from your cognitive and energetic field. Through meditation and/or shamanic work these energetic imprints and the thought forms behind them can be healed and transformed.

Shamanic Healing for Ancestral Imprints and Projections

Once we have an awareness of the role our ancestral imprints play in keeping us energetically and cognitively stuck, we can heal these imprints and projections through shamanic healing practices. It is important to note that just as we absorb or introject imprints from others through their projections, we also send these imprints out to others through our projections. As we have taken on negative energetic states, it is likely we have also sent them on to others. Not always do these projections do harm. The harm ensues when they are done in a repeated fashion to someone with whom we have a close connection and is open, based on familial, workplace or a friendship connection, to our energy. A projection might become embedded when the projection is of the same vibration as the other person's negative ancestral imprint such as with Suzy and Don. In the field of psychology we refer to this as a transference/counter transference phenomena or as projective identification. Historically this dynamic has been viewed as fertile ground for unraveling emotional distress; many books have been written to tease out the various levels of this phenomena. When a client projects one of her issues onto the therapist and this issue resonates with the therapist's issue, the therapist is likely to have a reaction, hopefully internally. Sometimes the therapist becomes snarled in the client's projection, becoming triggered by the client's comment, and responds from the pain and defensiveness of her wound, temporarily losing sight of who her client is, shrouded in the pain of her past. A skilled supervisor can assist the psychotherapist in sorting out the counter transference reaction. For instance, a client that feels/believes that no one is truly there for her shares this with the therapist and includes the therapist as another that has disappointed her by her lack of genuine care and support. The therapist, haunted by her mother's pronouncement that she is a failure and a disappointment for not being a more caring daughter, has a strong internal reaction. If triggered, the therapist might respond in a defensive manner, by reciting the myriad ways she has been there for her, totally missing the client's need to give voice to this deep pain. She could respond from a place of failure by telling the client that she is not the right person to treat her, thereby abandoning the client, actualizing the client's worst fears. Ideally the therapist would acknowledge and hold the client's pain regarding the lack of support she has found in her life by asking what she needs to feel more supported, tucking her own reaction away until she has time to be with it. This same dynamic often occurs among friends, family and coworkers. It is the origin of unresolved conflicts in a vast array of relationships.

The receiving of energetic projections of those with whom we work is heightened when doing shamanic work. For this reason, when I first begin a two-year shamanic training program, I have my students do six shamanic journeys to find protective guides in each of the six directions[13] and to learn from their spirit guides and power animals the vulnerabilities for which they most need protection. This is extremely important. When a shamanic practitioner works to remove and heal unneeded energies, it is important that the practitioner is well protected by their spirit guides and power animals so that they do not absorb any of the energy that they are removing. We are most vulnerable to taking on our client's energies when the energy being extracted is the same vibration as energies that are problematic to us; if we came from a fearful, anxious family as did our client, we are vulnerable to absorbing the fearful, anxious energy of the client without the protection of our spirit guides and power animals.

When doing a shamanic healing for the extraction of unwanted ancestral, cultural or karmic imprints, I first ask the client if they are ready to give up these energies. Some worry that if the energetic container, albeit negative and self-defeating, is removed, that they will dissolve into a million pieces. Others express a hesitation as the imprints feel like it is who they are. Expressed fears and concerns that there would be emptiness or they will not know who they are, are common. I tell clients with these trepidations that with the energy of others' imprints gone, you will be able to experience more of who you are, but since those aspects of the self are either lost from consciousness or buried deep within your being, you do not currently have access to them. A common apprehension is that one is failing her ancestors by no longer being willing to carry their emotional burdens. Actually the opposite is true. Our ancestors, for generations back, carry aspects of this burden and this burden comes with them into their next incarnations. Once this energy is healed and removed, then they are free of it, the client is freed of it, and all who come after will also be freed of this energetic burden. There is an energetic basis for the biblical statement that the sins of the father will plague his offspring for seven generations to come.

If there is hesitancy on the part of the client, I suggest that we do a shamanic journey to understand more clearly the nature of the unease. One needs to be clear that she wants to release the energy or her mind will just call it back. Once the client feels comfortable with releasing the ancestral, cultural or karmic burden, I have her lay down on a blanket. We smudge with sage, then I use incense and a sacred bowl to infuse my crystals with divine spiritual energy. I invite all of my and my client's spirit guides and power animals to be present for the healing. I request that the healing be in the client's highest good and just what they need for today. The latter is important as there can be a tendency to want to do more healing work than the client can energetically integrate.

I first run my hands over the client's energy field to feel for leaks, blocks, intrusions and whatever else might want to reveal itself to me. Then I work with a sacred, clear quartz crystal that helps to illuminate the energies that may be problematic. It is as if visions arise when the crystal is placed over certain aspects of the body presenting images of energetic blocks or past traumas.

As this occurs, I begin to feel the room fill with both my client's and my spirit guides and power animals. One of my spirit guides creates an energetic healing tent that is filled with divine energy, reminding me of the field hospitals on the TV show, *M*A*S*H*. Often I sense the presence of the ancestors standing in the field outside of my office, awaiting a healing for the painful energies that they have carried for years. As I am deeper into trance, the guides begin to work through me. I can sense the subtle energies move in and out of my being as their expertise is needed. Often the fierceness of my crocodile or the sea genii are the first to rip out the gross elements of the negative energy, but then other guides from the divine frequency realm move through me.

My client's guides and power animals also fill the room. They direct the healing, instantly knowing the energies in need of removal, to whom they belong and how to heal them. Sometimes the ancestral energy presents as a solid form, as was the case with Jack. This energy is pulled out intact and sent to guides for healing and transformation. As in Jack's case, often a deceased person to whom the energy belongs is present for the healing. Usually they have taken some of the client's energy and are here to return it to them in a healed form.

At times the energy presents as a very delicate web of energy. In these instances I feel the presence of one of my guides from the divine plane, Sherab Chamma, move into me as she delicately unravels and removes the web of energy. Often there are several layers to the energetic web. For instance, the dominant energetic imprint may be anger, but under it are layers of fear, hurt and shame, the anger serving as a protective cover for the more painful energetic states. It is common to find wounded parts of the client buried beneath this energetic web. These parts are removed and healed before they are brought back to the client's energy field. Sometimes aspects of the client that have been pushed out by the energies of another trail behind the client's energy field, waiting for the space to return. Other times a soul retrieval is needed to bring back lost parts of the soul.[14]

The most important aspect of the healing process of the ancestral, cultural and karmic energies is to see that these energies are healed, transformed and returned to whom they belong. Our goal is to restore as many beings as we can to wholeness. Merely tossing the energies aside not only pollutes the landscape with toxic energies looking for a new home, but also deprives others from becoming whole. It is in this wholeness that we can meet each other face to face in love and acceptance. Trust not only in one's guides, but in the client's guides is crucial as they know the nature of the wounding and what is needed for the healing to be beneficial. They also have the ability to trace the vibrations of the ancestral and karmic energies back to their rightful place.

After the ancestral, cultural and karmic energies are removed, healed and transformed, I fill the energy field of the client with divine healing energy and wrap her in an energetic bubble of divine healing energy. Then I journey with my guides and my client's guides to see if there is more work to do. The collective healing guides scan the dreambody to discern if there are more soul parts to be brought back and what healing work may be necessary for each part that was lost, buried, taken by another or pushed aside. After the soul parts have received a healing, they are blown into the client's heart and crown chakra. Spirit usually sends a special guide or protector for each of the soul parts so these spirit beings are blown in as well. The universe does not allow voids, so once energy is extracted, other energies need to be returned to fill the space left behind by the removed energies. Positive aspects of one's being are commonly restored as well in a healing. Traits such as hope and compassion can be pushed out by anger, judgment, and cynicism. As each soul part is healed, the natural state of this part is restored resulting in feelings of love and joy that had been, for the most part, absent from one's life.

During the shamanic healing, I am also mindful of retrieving any energies of projection that may be in the field of another. Healing energy is sent to those who took in the energy of projection from my client and the negative aspects of the projections are healed and returned to the place from which they originated. The majority of the negative energies that we either take in or send out are the negative emotions that we all struggle with such as anger, fear, judgment, envy, jealousy, shame, and greed—emotions that block us from our true heart. Often these energies are paired with hurtful words and actions that became embedded in the field. There are a continuum of imprints and projection from the relatively benign to a horrific level of toxicity. In the case of energies that are essentially dark or are aspects of another entity, a shamanic procedure called a depossession is used to remove this energy. Working with and understanding negative energetic states will be the focus of my next book.

I do not always share the energy of projection that my client launched from her own pain onto another. We still live in a cultural environment in which blame is a dominant force: "we are either right or we are wrong and there is someone at fault, someone to blame". For some the awareness that she might have sent her toxic energy to another will call back shame and self-hate and undo the work that was just done. Clinical judgment is often needed to determine what will facilitate a person's growth and well-being, and what will undermine the work that has been done. Again our spirit guides and power animals serve as a guide as to what should be shared directly and what should be revealed in a more general or obtuse way. They have the capacity to see the larger picture and more accurately discern where each person is in her healing journey. If I see that a client was raped and severely abused as a small child, I will not report this unless the client already has recalled this trauma. Instead I report that I healed and brought back a part that seemed to have been harmed, and in time that part will reveal what happened.

As we evolve in our understanding of how we as humans operate, we are able to see the web of energies that we carry from generation to generation, from our previous incarnations, and from cultural and societal imprints and belief systems. Gradually we discover how these imprints have clouded a true sense of who we are and watch in delight as who we truly are emerges. With an awareness of this understanding, the levels of self-hate, shame and blame that all too many of us carry fall away. An awareness of how we came to be who we are allows us to take responsibility for the changes that we need to make in order to walk squarely on our path without apology, judgment or blame of self or other.

It may appear to be a lot of work to keep track of all the musings in our mind and to look at the veracity of our feelings in a given situation before speaking or acting, but the benefits are enormous. We are freed from the emotional dramas and the continual upsets. There is ease and space in one's life to live in peace with the ability to delight in the little things that make life so special, little things that we might miss if we are slugging through the land mine of projections that reside in our mind and energy fields.

Part III

Understanding Our Karmic Imprints

Religious traditions and philosophers differ as to whether we experience multiple lifetimes or just one. Atheists, agnostics and practitioners of the three great religions that flowed from Abraham and Sarah—Christianity, Judaism, and Islam—believe that we are graced with a single lifetime. Hindus and Buddhists purport the existence of many incarnations. Whether you do or do not believe in multiple lifetimes or are not sure what to think, I invite you to approach this section with an open heart.

My openness to previous incarnations arose from an intuitive knowing that a place that I had never visited before was known to me. I do not recall being introduced to the concept of past lives before I first arrived in Malaysian Borneo straight from rural Indiana. Once in Borneo I had numerous *déjà vu* experiences and the overwhelming sense that the remote jungle village in which we had been assigned to live and work for two years was known to me. I felt as if I had come home and experienced such peace and joy living there. One-third of the people in the village were Chinese shopkeepers. As I got to know these gentle people and their customs and beliefs, I was introduced to the hypothesis that we live many lifetimes; they stressed the importance of accumulating good karma to carry from one life to the next. This insight provided an intellectual framework in which to house the intuitive knowing that grew daily from my felt experience.

One could write several books on what karma actually means, illuminating the various perspectives from a variety of cultures and religious traditions. Does karma mean that if one is a murderer in one lifetime that he will be murdered in the next? Or is the definition more expansive? For the purpose of better understanding the energetic dimension, I define the karmic energetic body in the following way: According to my power animals and spirit guides, we have access to the incredible wisdom that has accumulated through our various lifetimes. These life lessons flow within our consciousness as we move from one incarnation to the next as the soul evolves and grows. We absorb energetic imprints from these various lifetimes in a manner similar to the absorption of ancestral imprints. Some are a faint whisper that might be activated in a lifetime that holds similar energy streams. Some imprints are strong and provide the core foundation of who we are. Like our ancestral imprints, some karmic imprints are in need of healing while others are talents to be brought forward and shared.

The dreambody is a vibrational energy body that attaches in the front at our solar plexus and at the back around our kidneys.[15] It is the vehicle in which the vibration of every memory of every lifetime, including our current one, is stored. The dreambody houses the soul and is the vehicle through which our soul essence enters our body when we are born and carries our soul to other realms when our body dies. Those who do past life regressions have the ability to guide a person to the outer edge of the dreambody to access important information from previous incarnations that can clarify and illuminate certain longings, traits, gifts and skills as well as traumatic occurrences that might be negatively impacting one's life.

At this time of healing and transformation on the planet, the wisdom from other lifetimes is sorely needed as we seek a new evolved consciousness. In order to fully bring this information forward, it is important to remove and heal karmic burdens as well as cultural messages that provide the foundation for our prejudices and biases that have been carried from lifetime to lifetime. In addition, the need to remember and access the many gifts and talents that we have amassed over lifetimes and the wisdom we have garnered is crucial at this auspicious time. Through the rush to modernization, we have lost our ability to connect with and work with the elements, to listen to the teachings of the plants that can sustain and heal our bodies, and to live in harmony with the other beings with whom we share the planet. There is much knowledge that has been lost that needs to be remembered and reclaimed.

Chapter 8

Awakening to the Ancient Wisdom Within

When I was a small child, I loved a book with pictures of the children of the world. I was most drawn to the pictures of children from China. I asked my parents where China was and was told that it is on the other side of the earth. I spent the fourth summer of my life in the backyard digging a hole that would bring me to this magical far-off place that so called to me.

When I applied to the Peace Corps, I was aware that I had strong preferences as to where I would like to be stationed as well as places that I would prefer not to be sent. We were allowed to list these preferences, but there was no guarantee that these preferences would be honored. I pondered from whence these predilections arose since I had never been outside of the continental US. These musings were compounded by my decision to marry a man who had independently applied to the Peace Corps before we were engaged. Bob had a strong draw to northern Africa; whereas the idea of living in dry desert land held no appeal to me. The image that arose when I thought of going there was of oppression and death. There was nothing in my current lifetime that would account for such strong forebodings. In the late sixties the conditions in northern Africa were more stable than they were in Asia with the Vietnam War at its apex. My fiancé's draft board made the decision for us. Bob was rapidly working his way through the draft board's appeal process with denials at every phase. The Peace Corps responded by placing us in the first available training program, which sent us to Malaysia. Bob had studied in Tunisia and loved it there, but he would have been on his way to Vietnam before the start date for the training for Tunisia. Although he enjoyed his time in Malaysia, it never held the strong sense of being home as it had for me nor did he carry any desire to return. How does one explain such inclinations?

Energy streams arise within that feel strong yet appear to be disconnected from our current lifetime. We are haunted in our dreams by images that float by from far-off places, different eras and time periods. We feel drawn to explore certain parts of the world and feel a dread at the thought of visiting other areas. We meet people that we happily feel we have known forever and others to whom we feel an instant dislike or foreboding. Some attribute these various feelings to a karmic awakening.

I was raised in a conservative Christian Church in which the discussion of heaven and hell was a frequent topic. As a child, I spent hours trying to determine which actions or behaviors would get me into heaven, and which bad actions or behaviors would send me straight to hell. I tried to reconcile the teachings that stated that Jesus and God were all-loving, compassionate and forgiving with a god that would send one to hell for something bad. If one broke the Ten Commandments, would you automatically be sent to hell? Are all of us who told a lie or who had an adulterous affair condemned to hell? These questions haunted me throughout my entire childhood and into my college years. I was thrilled when I discovered that there were past lives as this meant one had many lifetimes to get it right.

Many occurrences are readily understood through the lens of other lifetimes; whereas many things go unexplained if one rules out previous incarnations. While in graduate school in psychology in the early seventies, there were numerous studies that attempted to establish the reasons why children from the same family were so different. Was it birth order or the genetic traits of each child that resulted in one child being smarter, better looking or more athletic than another? Why do some children grow up feeling that their mother or father preferred another sibling to them? And as hard as a parent might try, why is there a preference for one child over another? None of the studies shed any conclusive light as to why children with relatively the same genetic makeup and the same family environment are so different.

The family lore around my brother and my early childhood clearly foreshadowed who we were to become. Allegedly when my brother was naughty, my mother put him on a chair in time-out; he obediently sat there until granted a reprieve. He grew up to become a conservative banker. I, on the other hand, in the same circumstance would go rigid, slip from my mother's grasp and run into the street seeking my freedom. I went on to live a less than conventional life. My brother and I love each other and are close, but we are very different in ways that can only be explained through the various incarnations that made us who we are today. My mother used to comment that they do not know where I came from as I am not like anyone in the family. Fortunately, I was a dead ringer for my dad or a case might have been made for my being switched at birth. My felt sense is that my karmic influences are stronger than my ancestral ones. I grew up feeling outside of the family, not quite a part of it; nevertheless, I have come to understand that my family of origin was the perfect launching pad for my life's journey.

If we are open to accepting the possibility of previous incarnations, then many of these questions are answered through the understanding that each of us have had unique experiences through our various lifetimes. Some have had many lifetimes and carry both the wisdom as well as the suffering from various incarnations. Others have had fewer lifetimes, which often results in very different perspectives about reality. Some are born in an area of the world in which they had never lived before causing a more cautious or disoriented incarnation. Whenever I go to Asia, I feel at home and experience my heart opening and singing as I settle into the vibration of the land and customs there. When I return to the US, I feel as if I have hit concrete as I experience the energy here as dense, the spiritual energy of the land repressed through the genocide of its original inhabitants that treated the land as a sacred place.

We tend to incarnate into a family in which at least some of the family members are known to us. When I first held my son, I *knew* that he was someone that was well known to me. Not only did my heart sing with a mother's love, but also with a joy that someone that I had deeply loved was with me again. Sometimes we are born into a family in which there are one or more family members with whom we have challenging karma. In a shamanic journey, my guides told me that we come into each lifetime with something to manifest and something to heal. Often the conditions are established in a given lifetime to bring to light an issue that is ripe for healing. This explains why some have challenging and painful childhoods. It also sheds light on why some children are preferred by one parent over another as a result of a positive or conversely a negative connection from another life. There are also ancestral imprints that impact these preferences, particularly if a child reminds one of an abusive relative or on the other hand one's favorite grandparent. There are a multitude of reasons why each of us is uniquely who we are.

Bringing Forth What We Know

In addition to opening to the knowledge that each of us has accumulated through our karmic journeys, there is a source of knowledge to which each of us individually and collectively has access. Carl Jung wrote eloquently on the concept of the collective unconscious.[16] It is an aspect of consciousness in which intuitive wisdom and knowledge that has been stored throughout the ages is accessible to all. We can tap into the streams of consciousness from long ago or sense the subtle shifts in thought and mood throughout the modern world. This ability resides within us all, yet in the West, the development of intuitive and psychic gifts is at best ignored and more frequently derided as foolishness. By ignoring these gifts, we fail to utilize part of our brain and our being while we struggle to make sense of the many thoughts and images that permeate our consciousness.

Through shamanic journeying, meditation and the dream state we have the opportunity to glance into this rich well of experience and consciousness. As previously stated, my spirit guides underscored their understanding that we come into each lifetime with both a life purpose as to what we are to accomplish and learn, as well as what we are to heal from previous lifetimes. Sometimes the two are intertwined as what we are to heal provides the avenue for what we are to bring forward. It is often easier to work on what we need to heal when we have a clearer sense of our overall purpose and how our personal healing fits into this overall plan.

To get in touch with the richness of what we already know, we first need to learn to listen to ourselves. Most are aware of a voice or an intuitive knowing that often pops up as our first reaction to an idea, impression or suggestion. "Wow, this person has incredible energy," or "This person gives me the creeps." Sometimes this voice speaks out regarding large decisions. "This job has everything that I always thought that I wanted in a job. Why does it not feel right?" Many of us disregard the voice or inkling and turn to the rational mind. "I should not make snap judgments about people; I should not be so judgmental; I must be afraid of failing to be questioning taking this job." The rational mind or the *shoulds or beliefs* that we have been taught often override our initial instinct.

When I think back over my life, I am aware that for each major decision that I regret making, I ignored this internal voice of wisdom. Visually I recall the moment in which I allowed others' expectations, my sense of duty or my rational mind to veto what I knew intuitively to be my truth. I see where I was, who was with me and can even experience the inner sigh that I felt as I said yes to what I wanted to reject. Take a few moments to see if the same is true for you. Then for one week watch for that voice or intuition to arise. See how often it emerges and most importantly if you listen to it, or ignore and dismiss it. Often fears arise that tell us not to do something. Sometimes a deeply embedded voice of a parent or teacher steers us from our true heart. It takes time to distinguish our true voice from early teachings, imprints and our fears regarding growth and change. A meditation practice is a wonderful way to discern the origins of the various voices in our minds. Through the development of a relationship with our true voice or intuition, we begin to trust it and experience it as the gateway to our inner knowing and the collective unconscious. Power animals and spirit guides can help us to identify the various voices and intuitions that we encounter, telling us which to listen to and which to ignore.

Many are unaware that we can ask for guidance. If I have a question or concern that I am pondering, I set the intention in my morning meditation for clarity on the issue. From the stillness of meditation, the answer arises to my question. The same practice can also be used in the dream state. Before going to sleep, I often ask for guidance on a topic and either receive a dream that answers my question or awake in the morning with clarity on the issue.

Shamanic journeying is an excellent way to gather information from other realms. In the various workshops that I teach, I guide my students to do a shamanic journey to ascertain what they are to manifest and learn in this lifetime. We journey to find other lifetimes and important teachers from these lifetimes that will help us on our path. In addition to my previous lifetime in Matu, I have discovered several other lifetimes in which I was a healer, including one in which I practiced the dark arts of healing. Although it was painful to realize that I used healing energy in destructive ways, it has given me great insight as to how to work with negative energies in my current work. One student journeyed to find a lifetime in which she was a healer.

As the journey unfolded, she met the teacher who was to help her develop her gifts and talents. When this student returned home, she went online to Google the teacher's name to learn more about her. She expected the teacher to be in spirit form but was delighted to learn her teacher is alive and works as a healer in the exact place she was shown in her journey. She travelled to a foreign land to study directly with a former teacher who is on the earth at the same time she is. Not everyone discovers that they are to be a healer in this incarnation. Some find that they are to be artists, teachers, and businesspeople. One person received a clear and detailed message as to how to bring a shift in consciousness and work practice to the corporate world through consultation with his guides. Daily he converses with his guides as to how to run meetings, impact the work culture and find the perfect words to stress his point while having a challenging conversation. Creative thoughts and images flow to him from his guides as he embraces the larger context of his day-to-day work enabling his creativity to emanate from him with ease.

Shamanic journeying, meditation and dreamtime practices are not just for determining the large concerns regarding our life and purpose, but can be used continually to refine and redefine what we are to do next. Whenever I begin to feel stagnant in my work, I journey to ask what the next step on my path is or what should I be learning or doing to further my life path and purpose. In the beginning of my shamanic training, I was told that I needed to learn about the chakra system. I was unfamiliar with this, but as soon as I started to explore the chakra system and take workshops and trainings in this rich energetic system, I was aware that in a way this was all quite known and familiar to me. The courses reawakened what I already knew. Daily I receive interesting and enlightening information from my guides that enhances my life and work.

Countering the Dominant Paradigm

One of the great gifts of my time in Malaysia was to grasp the relative nature of reality. I quickly understood that the rituals and customs of a culture are what binds the culture together on the one hand, but at the same time, it is totally arbitrary. Most grow up in a community in which there are clear expectations of what is appropriate and what is not. As a child, we accept what we are taught as the truth and perceive the world through the lens of our families, teachers, culture, class and geographical location. The Unites States has been referred to as a melting pot of various ethnic and religious traditions. Some embrace the diversity of learning and working with people who are different than they are; whereas others strive to keep their cultural identities intact, and are fearful and distrustful of those who are in any way different than they are. The Civil War in the 1800s and the cultural wars in the 21st century speak to the challenges of navigating different beliefs, customs and cultures within one nation. Why is it that some of us champion diversity while others fight to keep their worldview pure and uncontaminated from any outside influence?

Before the advent of planes, ships, trains, cars, the Internet and television, we primarily stayed in the same area in which we were born. When I lived in Sarawak, a state in Malaysian Borneo, in the late sixties, it was the size of Texas with the population of Rhode Island. Fifty-two different languages and dialects were spoken in this vast and sparsely populated state. I learned an unwritten language that was spoken by a mere two thousand people. Many in Matu had not traveled beyond a few neighboring villages that one had the arm strength to row to as there were no roads, only rivers that wove majestically through the rain forest. It took two to three days, depending on the tides from the South China Sea, in a dilapidated Chinese boat called a launch to reach the nearest town where there were roads, buses and a few cars. Many had never made this journey. People stayed within their tribal groups.

Most of our karmic memories are of a tribal existence with a shared consciousness as to the nature of reality. The modern era is a small blip in the history of the world. Thus, there is an unconscious karmic pull to belong to a tribe. Sports facilitate this yearning. I live in Red Sox Nation, which is a shared identity for many who live in New England. We hate the Yankees because they win so much and feel smug to be Patriot fans as they win so much. The contradiction in this stance is ignored as a result of the collective reality we have created. The same can be said about the tribal reality of political parties. One party will openly condemn the other for the same actions that they championed the year before. Apparently, the tribal belief is that whatever we do is fine and whatever they do is wrong, even if they are the same thing. We live in a world that is formed by billions of people's individual realities that coalesce into tribal realities which are experienced as the true reality. With the advent of the Internet, multiple realities vie for prominence while denouncing other opinions and actual facts as fake news.

The daily bombardment of news that flows from alternate realities, which is substantiated by facts that are constructed to shore up one's reality, provides us with an exceptional opportunity to go inside to connect with what we really believe. The dominant reality that most heretofore lived under was viewed as the truth. With the dissolution of a coherent reality or narrative, we are uniquely situated to pause to listen to what we already know. There is a plethora of knowledge that each of us carries within that is just outside of the dominant frequency band of our consciousness. As we still our mind to listen to what we really feel and believe, the ancient knowledge that each of us carries within can surface bringing new understanding and wisdom to our daily lives. Why are we here on the planet, in this place at this time? What did I come here to learn and to do?

Many of us have inklings of what we want to do from an early age, but often are discouraged by the lack of practicality in our choice. We may not be introduced to the awareness that there are occupations that fit our interests. When I was a child, I had never heard of a psychologist or a shaman let alone knew what one did. I carried a vague notion that I wanted to "help people" but did not feel drawn to be a nurse or a teacher. Some are limited by the choices presented by our parents, teachers or community; others are made to follow the professional or business choices of our families. Some are deterred by their class, gender or race from pursing their dreams. All too often, we have not been allowed to dream and have been limited by the parameters of the choices that are placed in front of us. Rarely are we encouraged to study painting techniques in Bali or to follow a vision that we received in a journey to travel to Guatemala to study herbs with a native teacher.

Stored within each of us are caches of images from other lifetimes that hold clues for what we are to do in this lifetime. Perhaps we are to create a new form of community based on previous lifetimes of experience or a new agricultural method that was known to us thousands of years ago, but was lost over the ages. There is a wealth of information that we carry that goes beyond what has been historically recorded. Many believe that the early civilizations of Atlantis, the Mayans and the early Egyptians far surpass what we know today, particularly in the area of the capacity of the mind. It has been reported that the people of Atlantis[17] were able to gather in groups to psychically move large boulders with their minds; they were able to communicate telepathically. This ability was depicted in the latest *Star Wars* movie, *The Last Jedi*, in which Rey moved large boulders with her mind in order to allow the Resistance to escape annihilation. This is viewed as science fiction rather than a skill that can be developed. Rather than develop these aspects of our brain, our culture seems to be veering towards a highly computerized technological consciousness where we download volumes of information from our handheld devices, at times forgetting to think for ourselves. Yes, I must admit that my smartphone is never far from me and that there are many ways in which my life is made easier because of it. If this is the only way that we receive information, however, we are at risk of being both manipulated and limited by those who control the information that we receive. We have access to centuries of ancient wisdom that can arise from within if we take the time to pause and listen. As Malaysia and other developing nations struggle to find the balance between the ancient ways and the new, we must also find balance between technological advances that influence the information that we receive and our own intuitive knowing. Through validating intuitive knowledge as much as we do the information that we get from the Internet, our educational institutions and the news, we free ourselves to design a life of our own choosing.

Accepting Who We Are

If we accept the premise that we have had multiple lifetimes, then it follows that some of us have had more lifetimes than others. We have had a population explosion in the last few centuries, thus new souls have come to populate the planet. Those that have had many lifetimes, commonly referred to as "old souls", may have more wisdom than those that have had fewer incarnations on the planet, but they may also carry more suffering and wounds in their karmic imprint. Others who have experienced less time on planet earth may find modern industrialized life overwhelming and thus long for a sense of belonging that comes from strong ethnic and religious identification; they look for guidance, for someone to tell them what to do. There is the middle group that has a sense of mastery as to what life on earth is about and strive for power and recognition, often leaving a path of destruction in their attempts to reach the top. The soul progression of our incarnations over lifetimes is similar to developmental stages within each lifetime. We do not expect a child of three to understand how to maneuver life on her own; we give latitude to adolescents for their impulsive, defiant and reckless behavior. We acknowledge and expect those in their thirties and forties to be focused on their careers as they strive to create a successful life. As one ages, a subtle wisdom emerges at the same time as the energy to manifest the fruits of this sagacity wanes.

We live in a time in which we strive to emulate sports figures and movie stars. The media and the advertising industry tells us what to buy, what to wear, and what is in and what is not. It takes a strong person to be who they truly are, to counter the multitude of messages from the dominant culture and our families as to who we are to be. A major cause of depression is a loss of connection with our true self. Many delightful and joyous little beings have their sense of self drummed out of them by the third grade. When I was in my early thirties, I did not have a television as I discerned that I would never come to truly know myself while I had a little box broadcasting who I should be and what I should think. Each of us is unique based upon our karmic and ancestral lineages. We need to honor this rather than compare ourselves to others.

When I train others to become shamanic practitioners, some are shy about owning that they are healers; whereas others become over ego identified with this assignment. I emphasize that this is part of their karmic path in this lifetime. It does not make them more or less special than anyone else. It is what we agreed to do. Just as each of us has a unique contribution to make in the overall functioning of a community or society. There is no need to hide from our chosen work or to become overidentified with it. Just as it is important to own our ancestral gifts and talents, it is important to honor and further develop the gifts and talents from our karmic lineage. Sometimes our ancestral and karmic gifts dovetail, which makes for an easier path. Other times part of one's soul's evolution is to override obstacles placed in our way by families, our culture or gender in order to own our karmic path.

Some people are afraid to honor their gifts and talents as they fear that it might set them apart from others, the desire to fit in overriding one's internal yearnings. If one comes from a family of musicians in which one is encouraged to own her musical talents, then the convergence of the ancestral and karmic imprints fosters the development of her life purpose. If one with musical talents is born into a family that has no interest in music and even spurns the pursuit of this gift, then this potentially gifted musician will need to find a mentor or another form of support to ripen this talent. In the first example an aspect of her life lesson is to take advantage of the support that is offered, to allow herself to fall into a warm supportive environment in which she can blossom. Perhaps she has had several lifetimes in which she was not supported to own her passion and her life lesson is to receive this, to heal the pain of this lack. The latter case speaks to the challenge that many face in pursuing their ambitions when it goes against the wishes of one's family, and in some instances, one's ethnic and religious community. Many wilt under this pressure and acquiesce to their family's wishes. There is no right or wrong answer in this situation. Perhaps the lesson to be learned in this lifetime is to consent to another's wishes after lifetimes of forcing one's will on others; while for another it might be to finally assert one's will and own one's passion and path. One needs to get quiet and go inside to discern the correct choice for this lifetime. If we still the mind in order to listen to our inner wisdom, without rational thought or the force of ego undermining the connection with our true voice, the right answer will arise from a deep space within.

Taking on New Lessons

We come into each lifetime with something to heal and something to learn and manifest. We would all like to think that we came here for a grand purpose and for our life to have meaning, but sometimes we come to learn an important life lesson that has eluded us in previous lifetimes. Many with whom I have worked over the years have lamented the hardship and suffering in their lives or have negatively compared themselves to others and have felt shortchanged. They become angry or bristle when I ask them to explore if there have been important life lessons in their experiences. There is a belief in the West that life should run smoothly and that one should not have to encounter pain and suffering. In Buddhism, there is an acceptance that suffering does exist. We all get sick and die, we lose those we love, our life does not always turn out as we had dreamt, our kids do not do what we want them to—the list goes on and on. Although Buddhists acknowledge that suffering does exist, they purport that the degree to which we suffer is optional. Many grow their suffering by attaching to it and affixing it as a core part of one's identify. If, however, we are able to see each adversity, loss or challenge as an opportunity to learn and grow rather than as a punishment, our suffering decreases tenfold and the progression of our soul's journey is enhanced.

Most often we are born into a family, culture and economic class that will foster the growth that our soul needs. Many great leaders, such as Martin Luther King, Jr., Nelson Mandala and Gandhi, were born into poverty in countries that perpetuated class and racial injustice. Each went on to radically change their respective country for the good. For eons there has been economic disparity throughout the world. One theory purports that before we cycle off the earth plane, one must experience all that there is to experience.[18] Thus each of us will have the opportunity to be rich and famous while also poor, oppressed and abused. The issue is not the conditions to which we are born, but what we do with them. There are plenty of tales of one who is born to a rich and powerful family only to struggle throughout life, often experiencing a tragic death, just as there are accounts of those who have persevered in the face of difficult situations.

Often the growth path is in the relational realm. There may be a person with whom we have had several challenging lifetimes and are once again given the opportunity to understand, heal and change the dynamic that has haunted each of us throughout the life cycle. One may have had a series of lifetimes in which he was a bully and may be presented with the circumstances to learn the pain of this practice. Some lifetimes are about learning resiliency or compassion; others about living with physical or mental challenges or caring for someone who is incapacitated.

Take a moment to review your life. Are there themes that come up again and again, such as difficulties with anger or maintaining connections? Do you get bored at work and frequently change jobs, never feeling fulfilled? Do you always back down in a fight or are you the one who storms out issuing ultimatums? Are there some things that were challenging in your youth that you now do with ease? You may be surprised at all you have already learned and what you have accomplished. Most of us do not appreciate or even acknowledge the progress we have made on our soul's journey.

Compassion is the most important quality to bring to the acceptance of who we are. I have discovered in my many years of doing healing work that one cannot fully heal unless one cultivates a sense of compassion for oneself, for all the struggles, mistakes and missteps that have occurred thus far in this life. If one sits in judgment of oneself, then there is a harsh energy that prevents the love and joy that is within each of us to flourish and manifest. Again, if we look at our mistakes and failures as opportunities for growth and teachings, there need not be judgment. Even if we make the same mistake repeatedly, be patient as this means that there is a deep healing that is needed which has eluded us thus far. Ask what it is that I need to know so that I can let this hurtful pattern release. Less effort often brings better results; put space around a problem or issue until the clarity that is needed arises. We are used to instant results and feedback, but deep change may take time. We do not put a seed in the ground and expect that the next day it will bear fruit.

Equally important is to develop a sense of compassion and equanimity for others. There is a tendency to perceive others through our own lens rather than see them as they truly are. If we were taught that hard work is the most important thing in life and meet someone who believes that enjoying life is the key to happiness, do not criticize the other person for being lazy; rather embrace that they have a different way of experiencing life. You might even question if it would be good for you to play a bit more and work a bit less. We can learn from how others approach life if we are not fixed in seeing them from our set perspective. To truly grow and be open, it is helpful to bring a level of wonder and openness as to how we think and experience reality and from this place there is space to allow the other to be who they are.

Repaying Karmic Debts

The word karma is often thrown around with little understanding of its true meaning. When a person is angry or feels betrayed by someone, I have often heard them comment, "They are going to have a big karmic payback for this one." There is the notion that if we do something wrong or hurtful that we will in some way pay for it by having the same thing done to us in the same way. I have even heard people justify their neglect and prejudice against those who are suffering, by believing that they karmically deserve it. This is not how karma works; it is much more complicated.

The karma that we accumulate, both positive and negative, is part of our soul's journeys, our life's lessons. If we were mean or destructive towards someone in a previous lifetime, it does not necessarily mean that they will return the favor now. Most commonly karmic debts are repaid through acts of kindness. If we stole from someone in another incarnation, perhaps in this lifetime we will be generous towards this person, not really understanding why we are pulled to have such an open and generous heart towards them. We may live a life of service and give to others to make amends for the harm that we have done in another lifetime.

In actuality, the harm that we do in one lifetime lives in our karmic energy body until that energy is healed and transformed. If we have had one or more lifetimes in which greed was the motivating principle, then the vibration of greed will live in our energy body, hanging out there as this pesky problem that can rear its ugly head just when we least expect it. We might struggle with the notion of charitable giving, believing that we should be generous, but in reality, feel as if we need to keep all the money that we can. We might draw business partners to us that are greedy, awakening our own struggle with money, perhaps evoking fears that the other person will cheat us, as buried within us is the tendency to cheat others. If we have had lifetimes of either being abused or of abusing others, this energetic pattern will live in the energy body drawing abusive people and situations to us until we finally deal with the pattern of abuse in our karmic history. Often if we ignore a dominant pattern over several incarnations, we might have a lifetime in which we have no choice but to face the power of an abusive imprint by living through abuse at the hand of another or abusing another to the extent that we are incarcerated for it. We are given opportunities to more benignly heal challenging imprints, but eventually if we fail to do this, we may experience a more direct re-experiencing of the harm we have done to others or to our own person.

Often, we are called upon to repay debts of kindness and support by caring for another as we were cared for. It does not always mean that we will take care of the same person in the same way that we were regarded, but it does mean that we may go out of our way to do for another in a similar manner in which someone was kind to us. Disasters, whether man-made or acts of nature, afford amazing opportunities for people to care and support one another and often bring out the best in us.

Each of us carries vibrational imprints from previous incarnations. Some are strong positive traits such as kindness, fearlessness, strength, perseverance and resiliency. Other imprints are in need of healing such as healing the vibration of envy. In some instances, we have had a traumatic lifetime and perhaps a horrendous death in which part of our soul essence remains behind. How to heal the trauma from other lifetimes is explored in the next chapter.

Chapter 9

Healing and Transforming Karmic Imprints

Karmic imprints can hold one back from pursuing one's path. When I begin a new shamanic training program, there is often some fear among the participants regarding opening to the path of a shaman. One of the first journeys that we do is to a lifetime in which we were happy and successful doing healing work. Next we journey to a lifetime in which practicing shamanism brought harm, banishment or even death. During the Spanish Inquisition, which began in the 15th century and lasted into the early 19th century, nine million healers were tortured and killed. Many, who have been healers in previous incarnations, have chosen to be on the planet at this time to assist in the planetary shift in consciousness and to retain the most positive aspects of ancient healing practices; practices that honor our connection to the earth and the elements, and to the wisdom that is available to us through guidance from the spirit world. In order to fully embrace this task, we must heal and clear any lifetimes in which our work brought suffering or death.

My shamanic teacher, Ismail Daim, and my teacher from the Bön Buddhist tradition, Tenzin Wangyal Rinpoche, both speak of demons and evil spirits. To be certain, there are evil spirits that can threaten to destroy our very being, but encounters with these beings are rare. According to these wise men, the vast majority of evil spirits or demons arise from the negative emotional states of anger, jealousy, greed, envy, hate, self-doubt, shame and fear. These negative emotional states can destroy the very fabric of our being whether one practices shamanism or not. Many in the West view these negative emotional states as part of our basic nature that needs to be tamed and controlled rather than as energetic winds that can be understood, healed and transformed. When one works as a shamanic practitioner, fear is often the most debilitating of these demons. Fear makes one vulnerable to attacks by negative energetic states; like a magnet, fear draws to us that which we most dread. The light is always more powerful than the dark and there is always light within even the most negative energetic states. Before one can safely pursue a shamanic path, lifetimes in which one's work brought harm or death must be healed. The pain of torture or an unjust death is like a thorn in the soul and carries the negative vibration of the harm that was done.

Students have discovered that they were hanged, burnt at the stake, eviscerated, imprisoned for the rest of their lives or shunned and banished from the community as they journeyed into a traumatic lifetime while working as an indigenous healer. For some, the fear from these experiences stays within the vibrational layers of the energy field; for others part of their soul essence is frozen and left behind, in need of a soul retrieval. It is important to acknowledge the terrifying experiences while also deeply taking in that somehow one's soul essence survived this ordeal to live another life. This knowledge helps to release the energy of the trauma. Some learned that they were able to survive horrific assaults by utilizing practices that they knew. With the support of their guides, they left their bodies to travel in the spirit world to a place in which they were safe negating the torturous aspects of their death.

Healing Past Life Traumas

The shamanic practices that one uses to heal past life traumas are the same for any other type of healing. Energy work and extraction can remove the vibrational threads of fear and terror from the field and transform this negative energetic state into positive energy. Often it is necessary to do a soul retrieval to heal and bring back a part of the soul that was so injured in another lifetime that it stayed behind. When I do a past life soul retrieval, I experience myself as dropping through many vibrational layers finally landing in another time and place. The spirit guides of the person with whom

I am working take me to the place where the soul is trapped. A healing is done for this part before bringing it back.

People often wonder what the indications are that one might need a past life healing. If one is terrified of heights and is afraid to climb mountains, go across high bridges or into the upper floors of skyscrapers, this may be the result of a past life in which one was pushed or fell off of a mountain or bridge. This fear alerts one to the fact that a healing is needed. If the soul essence transitioned to the other realms upon impact, then it is possible to heal and release the terror from this fall through energy work. But if part of the soul stayed behind, it is necessary to perform a soul retrieval. In the West we do not discuss or fully comprehend that part of our soul can fragment, split off or stay frozen at the site of a traumatic occurrence that results in death. We often pray that the soul will safely make its way to heaven or into the light, but we are unaware that there is a need to call upon the deceased person's guides to gather up the various soul parts before transitioning to the next realm.

Most heal past life trauma through situations in our current life. We choose a family that is ripe with experiences from which we learn and heal. If we have had lifetimes in which we were anxious and fearful, we might choose a family that is fearless. We might choose to overcome our fear of heights by being born in a mountainous region or to a family that loved to skydive and bungee jump. We might choose a family that is so filled with fear, that we experience how debilitating and pointless it is to spend one's life absorbed in this energy, that we detach from the fear-based energy. Others might absorb the fear-based energy, taking on the healing of this energy as the soul's life work. When we resolve and heal major emotional and energetic states in this lifetime, we also heal them from our previous incarnation and for incarnations to come.

Occasionally someone will come to see me with the assertion that they have felt traumatized—as if part of them was missing—

their entire life, yet there is no known event in this lifetime to account for this feeling state. Oscar, a thin somewhat frail man in his late twenties, came to see me with such a claim. There was little in his current life that would explain how he felt. During a soul retrieval for Oscar, I found myself falling through layers of energy until I saw myself standing on the rim of an open grave of many bodies. There was a golden sacred light surrounding the area that initially blinded me to what was before me. As my eyes adjusted, I realized that the grave was not just of skeletons, but also of soul parts. Oscar's guides then told me that these are the souls of those who were tortured and killed at Auschwitz. Many of the soul essences left before death, as the conditions were so horrific and dehumanizing, but others partially stayed with their bodies to the end. Oscar's guides alerted me to his soul part and we brought it out for a healing in order to bring it back to Oscar. Before I came back with Oscar's healed soul part, I knew that I could not leave the other souls there and called on all of my guides and the guides of all the souls who were there to come to do a healing and to unite the soul part with the rest of the soul, wherever it might be. Often when a soul has been as horrifically traumatized as these concentration camp victims were, the soul fragments are not able to fully transition to the next realm until the trauma has been released and the soul made whole. The energetic density of the trauma often keeps the soul fragments frozen at the site of the trauma. Hundreds of shamanic practitioners worked around the clock to attend to the victims of 9/11 in order to bring healing to their traumatized souls.

Sometimes one is not even aware that there has been a past life trauma until confronted with a trigger that forces one back into the traumatic state. Rosa is the daughter of good friends of mine who live out of state. Rosa is a delightful young woman that works as a psychotherapist and had attended some of my shamanic classes. Although she experienced anxiety in her life, it was not so debilitating as to interfere in the normal functioning of her life. Rosa was happily married and had recently given birth to a beautiful baby. Shortly after the birth of her baby, I received reports from her parents that Rosa was having a very challenging time and was unable to go back to work as planned. Then I learned that she and the baby had moved in with her aunt as she was unable to fully care for the baby. The next report stated that she was in day treatment for postpartum depression at a major psychiatric hospital. Medication had not helped her condition; Rosa was now receiving electric shock therapy (ECT).

Her mother came to visit. I invited Rosa, her new baby and her mother over for brunch. I was horror-struck when Rosa walked into my home. She was pale, thin and barely able to speak. Rosa held the baby as if the baby were a stuffed animal. It took half an hour for her to change the baby's diaper, staring off into space clearly unaware of the crying baby before her. After brunch, we went for a walk. As Rosa's mother pushed the baby in a carriage, I attempted to talk with Rosa. Energetically I felt as if I was walking alongside a body that did not have a being inside it. I was unsuccessful in engaging Rosa in conversation. I had experienced people as being barely present after ECT, but wondered if it might be more than this. After all, her condition had deteriorated to the point that ECT was necessary.

I asked if I might do a journey to discern what might be at the root of Rosa's condition. I told Rosa and her mother that I sensed a soul retrieval might be necessary. We made a time a few days later when her mother was able to drive her to my office as it was not safe for Rosa to drive.

During the journey, my spirit guides and power animals first took me to Rosa's home where she had had a home birth. Although the birth was a challenging one, Rosa did not remember it at all. In the journey, I found her standing in the corner of the room frozen in terror, but there did not appear to be anything upsetting in the scene before her other than the fact that Rosa was in active labor. I was then informed that this was a past life issue. After dropping through several layers, I found myself in Imperial Russia during the time period when male physicians were just beginning to deliver the babies of the aristocracy rather than a midwife as had been the custom. Apparently the physician did not know how to deliver a baby. I watched in shock and revulsion as the physician attempted to pull the breech baby out with forceps utilizing the utmost violence and force. The baby came out in pieces while Rosa screamed in pain and horror. The violence of his actions tore Rosa's womb; she bled out, but not before viewing the desecrated body of her baby.

My spirit guides did a healing for this past life part of Rosa, her poor baby and the part of Rosa that stood petrified in the corner of her current home. While they did these healings, my power animals and I did an energetic clearing of Rosa's energy field and of the baby's as well, removing the traumatic energy of this violent assault so that there was room for the healed soul parts to return to the energy body of both the baby and the mother. After the clearing and healing work was completed, my guides brought the healed baby into the light and to the other side. I then blew the two parts of Rosa's soul into her heart and crown chakras. As soon as I rattled around Rosa to seal the energy within her field, Rosa sat up, gave me a big smile and said, "I'm back." Her mother wept with relief.

The next day, Rosa returned to the day treatment program to tell them what had happened. Thankfully, they believed her and did not think her psychotic for relating such a tale. Rosa told me that they could see that she was fine and thus could not argue with her rendering of events. Her ECT appointments were cancelled and they immediately began to taper Rosa off the medications. Rosa and the baby moved back home as Rosa no longer needed help caring for the baby. She was back at work the next week. She, the baby and her husband are thriving; the previous lifelong anxiety that Rosa had experienced was greatly reduced to the point that it is no longer an issue for her.

Naturally I am curious as to whether past life birth trauma might be one of the causes of postpartum depression and psychosis. In Rosa's case concerning the traumatic past life experience, she had a moment before she died in which she witnessed the terrible shock of her dismembered baby. She dissociated at the trauma of this. A part of Rosa's soul essence left her body, the terror and pain of what was before her being too much to bear. Since the universe does not like a vacuum, the energy of the trauma in the room filled the space where part of Rosa's soul had been. The horrified part that had stayed frozen at the death scene was at the outer edge of Rosa's dreambody, but the terror was strong enough to result in an underlying anxiety that ran through Rosa's energy body. In this lifetime, Rosa was adamant that she wanted to have a home birth with a midwife. This strong feeling undoubtedly arose from the trauma of death by a physician, this faint inkling influencing her preferences. When Rosa went into active labor, the frozen, terrified and dissociated part of her moved into the dominant frequency band and was unable to function. One of the key elements in healing and bringing this part back was in assisting the soul part to realize that she was now living in another time and place with a happy and healthy baby, and that she was needed to come back to love and nurture this baby. As fanciful as this story might appear, it does illustrate the power of our energetic being to hold energetic strands that influence who we are and, in some cases, are in need of healing for the soul to be whole.

War

War is undoubtedly more responsible for the fragmenting and breaking of the soul than any other single activity. War also imprints the soul in such a major way that it can take several lifetimes to heal. It is my belief that serving in combat is so traumatic that one inevitably experiences soul loss while absorbing the violence, rage and fear from a battle in which one is asked to kill and perhaps be killed. This violence and rage travels home in the energetic field, often expressed through acts of violence against oneself, one's family or in other self-destructive ways such as addiction. The trauma of war often is unconsciously and energetically shared with those in the family passing this ancestral imprint from generation to generation. The energy of war may also become part of one's karmic soul essence and travel from one lifetime to the next. Killing a person and the fear of being killed is a significant event and impacts the core of the soul essence. Some may heal this by working for peace or having future lives of service. Others may become entrenched in the energy of war and spend repeated lifetimes as a warrior. The energy of battle is so strong that it pulls one to re-experience war until all aspects of it are understood.

A Vietnam War veteran came to see me for a soul retrieval. Bill had served as a medical evacuator. He flew into war zones on a helicopter to pick up the dead and those who were in the process of dying. Bill reported that many men died in his arms with their eyes locked with his. Bill confided that it felt as if he had carried the energy of those that died in his arms with him since his time in Vietnam. He believed that it was finally time to release them. Since Bill returned home in 1968, he has suffered from post-traumatic stress disorder. He has been haunted by images of the carnage, death and destruction that he witnessed there for his entire life. Bill has been prescribed psychotropic medications to ease his symptoms; however, this left him feeling foggy and not himself. Relationships have been hard to sustain; he is in his fourth marriage. He dreamt of starting a healing center for veterans of war utilizing alternative healing methods such as meditation, yoga and Tai Chi.

Bill's father had served in WWII. He was in the unit that liberated Auschwitz. Bill grew up terrified of his father as he was angry and violent. Both Bill and his father had been given the role of tending to the dead and dying. When I began Bill's healing with an energy clearing, his father's energy was plastered over his field. The anger and grief that his father carried from the war had been energetically passed onto Bill and felt like a brittle, crunchy plastic cover. As a draftee, Bill could have been assigned to any number of jobs. Perhaps the strength of this energy in his field drew him to be assigned to care for the dead and dying as this is often how things work. During the energy work, I found a number of souls hanging on around his shoulder; they were afraid to let go after finally finding a safe haven. Many who have served in war zones wonder, at times, if they are actually dead, left to wander in the hell of war for an eternity. Some who have died are not aware that they have, aimlessly roaming the battlefield. Even after physically returning home, many are still haunted by images of war forced to meander in the hell realms of this dehumanizing experience. Some of the soldiers hung onto Bill, unsure if they were alive or dead. My guides did a healing for them and sent them into the light.

As I journeyed in the soul retrieval part of the healing, I found numerous parts of Bill that had been lost in the war zone as well as parts of his energy that his father had taken. His father had come home an empty shell of himself and unconsciously drew on Bill's energy to survive. The brittle crusted energy that Bill had carried of his father's was healed and sent back to his father in exchange for the energy that he had taken from him. One of the tragic aspects of extreme soul loss is that one spends his life looking for a way to become whole. Some unconsciously draw on others' energies, others turn to addictions, while for others their energy field is so filled with the traumatic energy that there is not space for the soul to return; the constant bombardment of the trauma consumes them.

That Bill carried the ancestral imprint of his father's war experience was apparent, but I was curious to learn if there was a karmic imprint as well. As I journeyed on this, I learned that Bill had other lifetimes as a warrior. He had agreed to come back to be of service in the war as a way to make retribution for previous lifetimes in which he had harmed others on the battlefield. He chose a family that would provide the environment for him to be on this path. Bill also had agreed to help other veterans to heal from their soul-shattering experiences as part of his soul's path. As difficult as this lifetime has been, Bill chose it to heal his karma from previous lives as a warrior and to create a refuge for those with similar wounds.

The karma accrued in being a warrior is not only about what one has done to others, but also what it does to one's core essence. It is through compassion for oneself and for what one has experienced that the healing of the soul can occur. When our hearts are open and loving, lifetimes of negative actions can be healed. Healing karma is not about doing to another what was done to you; this only furthers the negative karmic cycle. It is not about payback or revenge for those who have harmed us or who we have harmed. Rather it is about healing the negative patterns that have been repeated throughout many lifetimes.

Understanding Our Karmic Imprints

It is easy to grasp the karmic implications of war. People are harmed, souls are shattered and the energy of battle permeates the energy field occupying the space that the soul once filled. Violent death by natural disasters, murder, accidents or other traumatic occurrences are understandable as well from a karmic perspective. There are, however, more subtle imprints from more ordinary times that are in need of healing if we are to move fully into a heart-centered awareness. It is sometimes difficult to discern the difference between ancestral and karmic imprints. Often they are intertwined as we choose incarnations that lay the groundwork for the soul's healing and path as Bill's did. Sometimes there are character traits that bleed through from one lifetime to the next; some are strengths and others hold us back from our true potential.

Each of us has our own personal struggles, often unknown to those around us. Gerri, a young attractive woman, struggled with a profound sense of inadequacy. As with many, there were minor incidents which one could point to as the origins of her feelings of worthlessness, but none that could explain the extent to which she carried the burden of this feeling. Her parents were moderately successful and had supported her throughout her early years, trying to help her with her shyness, refusal to try new things and to take risks. Gerri had spent a number of years in therapy trying to tease apart and understand the cause for these feelings. When I first did energy work for her, I could sense the heaviness of these energies and how deeply entrenched they were, going down to the core or root of her being. There was also a curious dark underbelly to this weighted energy.

During the soul retrieval journey, I descended through many layers to a lifetime in which she was a servant for a very wealthy family in China in the 16th century. Nothing that she did was good enough; she was regularly beaten for the slightest infraction. Her life was not a long one and she died broken and alone. A healing was done for her in this lifetime and this part of her was brought back. I was drawn to another lifetime as the journey continued. In this lifetime she was a male merchant in England during the late 17th century. In this incarnation, Gerri was obsessed with rank and class. He tried everything to improve his status, even stooping to harm and cheat others to get ahead. He died lonely and unloved.

Gerri's guides then shared with me that there had been an alternating pattern of lifetimes in which Gerri was brutally treated for minor mishaps, and lifetimes when Gerri tried to prove her worth on the backs of others. In this incarnation, Gerri had chosen relatively loving and accepting parents that had the means to be emotionally and financially supportive of her in order to begin to unravel the negative karmic patterns that went from one lifetime to the next. My guides then told me that we needed to heal the collective lifetimes of being treated so horribly countered by lifetimes in which she tried to overcompensate for her feelings of inadequacy by at times being cruel herself. The energy of cruelty was vibrationally in her field from those lifetimes in which she was abused. It was so strong that it either drew others to her who were cruel to her or she expressed this negative energy through her own acts of malevolence. At the root chakra, which represents our foundation as well as our sense of trust and safety, was the energy of inadequacy that was so strong that others assumed she was incompetent and treated her poorly for it. Once I had a better understanding of the complexity of the very entrenched energies in her field, it was easier to remove and heal them therein making space for the healed soul parts from numerous incarnations to return.

Gerri's situation illustrates how the soul can karmically become stuck in a negative pattern, trying lifetime after lifetime to shift the dynamic only to become further entrenched in it. The essential ingredient for healing a repetitive karmic pattern is to have compassion for oneself. We live in a culture in which we are either right or wrong. If we are wrong, then we are to blame. Many of us blame ourselves for negative emotions, and in the extreme, become self-hating and act in ways that call in the opposite of what we want to manifest, strengthening the negative cycle rather than healing it. If one has a problem with jealousy or envy, there is a tendency towards self-blame for these feeling states, or alternately, rage at the one who is provoking the feelings of jealousy. Instead of living a life engulfed in the torturous energy of jealousy, one needs to consider that there is a reason that one is always plagued by jealousy. With this understanding, the compassion is free to flow to begin the healing process. Without an awareness of the strength of ancestral and karmic imprints to impact how we feel and perceive reality, it is easy to blame oneself for feelings that are experienced as out of control.

Unlike Gerri who chose a loving environment to heal her past life wound, most of us choose an incarnation that calls us to confront head-on the issue that we came to heal. In the case of jealousy, one might choose an incarnation where other children were favored and received special treatment. Unfortunately, once an energetic pattern is firmly entrenched in our energy field, this energy tends to attract folks who will vibrate with this energy. One might go through a series of relationships in which the partner cheats. Or one might choose someone who is also very jealous; the two playing out the dramatic dance of suffering over each encounter the other has with a person who might be a potential love object. They torture each other with this jealous dance until one of them finally leaves or becomes physically ill. Extreme negative emotional states can weaken the immune system.

Usually the conditions are sufficient in one's current life to have the past life trauma healed through the issues that are presented in this life. A person that was plagued with strong feelings of jealousy in previous incarnations might choose a family in which she is overlooked in favor of the other children in the family. The healing of the wounded aspect of her soul and the removal of the strong energy of jealousy from this lifetime have the potential to heal not only this incarnation, but also the previous lifetimes in which she was tormented with feelings of inadequacy and jealousy. Occasionally the energy from the initial life event that created the extreme jealous state is so strong that a past life soul retrieval is necessary.

The Perils of Delving into Previous Lifetimes

There is much to be learned from our previous incarnations, but it is important not to delve so deeply into our past lives that we lose touch with the richness, meaning and purpose in our current incarnation. If we come into each lifetime with things to heal from another incarnation as well as things to manifest, it is important to also keep focused upon what we are to manifest. It would be too arduous a task to take on the healing of different issues from multiple lifetimes at once as this would interfere with what we are to accomplish and learn in the here and now. There is a reason that we do not easily remember our previous lifetimes. It is so we can be fully present in this one.

Focusing on past lives can be a way to escape the reality and problems of one's current existence. Skilled practitioners can accompany the client, with the help of power animals and spirit guides, to both explore relevant past life traumas while linking them to this current incarnation and the problems that one might have in the present. In our addiction-driven culture there is a tendency to be addicted to everything from drugs and alcohol to Facebook, Twitter and one's past lifetimes. It is important as we explore past life issues that we stay focused on the aspect of our life that we came here to heal and not become lost in the fascination with all of our previous incarnations.

I have had people come to see me that are certain that all of their difficulties in this lifetime are the result of past life events. Each issue in their life must be the result of a past life trauma. I have asked them to consider that there might be a link in this incarnation that is connected to a past life issue, but often there is a denial that there are any issues or problems. Sometimes the pain in this lifetime is so intense that the psyche does not allow it to come to awareness. Without acknowledging the difficulties in the present and being willing to heal issues from this lifetime as well as past lifetimes, it is not possible for past life healings to be complete. It is analogous to attempting to bring back a part that was beaten as a child to one who is in a marriage in which one is currently being beaten. The soul part will not agree to return to the same situation from which it left or to one in which the same vibration of harm is still occurring.

Malcom had difficulty finding and maintaining intimate relationships. Although he had had a brief therapy in which relational issues with his parents were explored, he found the therapy unhelpful claiming that his relationship with his parents was fine. Malcom also denied that there had been any significant event from his adolescence that might account for his difficulty in finding women to date and partner. He was convinced that his difficulties were related to previous lifetimes and wanted to do shamanic journey work to uncover and heal these lifetimes. I taught Malcom to journey so that we might explore together what was problematic from the past. In his journeys he discovered lifetimes in which he was Antony to Cleopatra, Anne Boleyn to King Henry, and Sir Lancelot to Guinevere. He believed from his journeys that he had experienced these great loves and had been unable to find a suitable mate in this lifetime as none could match the intensity and passion of his previous incarnations. I did not remind him that some of these relationships did not turn out so well. My journeys found some heartbreaking rejections that energetically predispose him to difficulties with intimacy. Malcom felt that my journeys did not ring true, but left aglow with the information from his journeys that once he had been well loved.

I never saw Malcom again. Hopefully Malcom's journeys gave him the confidence to engage in a meaningful relationship, but I fear that most likely it will give him an excuse not to try. It is possible that he did experience painful rejection and may have used mechanisms for coping that kept him away from confronting and healing this pain. It is an arduous task to visit some of the most difficult aspects of one's life, whether from this lifetime or a previous one. This is particularly true when a great wounding occurred in childhood. Children do not have the emotional capacity to understand what is happening to them, experiencing abuse, bullying and neglect as a blow to the psyche with scant psychic structures to process and understand the pain that has befallen them. Most dissociate from these traumatic experiences, erasing them from conscious memory, but the energetic imprint remains in the energy body, pulling for opportunities for reenactment so that the trauma can arise to consciousness to be healed. Given that there is most often an energetic link of pain from one's current lifetime that resonates with the lifetime in need of healing, it is necessary to acknowledge this energetic pattern so that it can be healed and transformed as well.

As Westerners, there is a tendency to want instant gratification. If there is a ball of string that is entangled in a mass of knots, there is a tendency to throw the string away rather than take the time to gently untie the various strings that are knotted and entwined. We want quick fixes and most are not as lucky as Rosa was to have her issue be so easily resolved. There is so much complexity as we weave together the vibrations of our past lives, our ancestral line with the current messages from the dominant culture. Often we carry thoughts and beliefs that hold the various energies that we want healed and released in place. Many of the thoughts and beliefs that keep us encased in negative energetic states are the result of cultural, ethnic, religious and spiritual beliefs. Many of these beliefs keep us from our true heart. The immigrant or person who is different from us that we fear may be from where we once lived and thrived. Once we can grasp the vibrational and energetic foundation of our being, we can see that energetically we are one with all that is and that we are part of the same vibrational fabric. Understanding will dawn that as we war with others we are also at war with our peaceful heart. In time, we will grasp that we are part of the same whole and that when one of us suffers, we all suffer.

Part IV

Cultural Imprints: The Lens through Which We See

There are many components that comprise a cultural imprint; it is not monolithic in nature. Our ethnic and racial makeup influence the traditions in which we participate, the way we speak, the clothes we wear and the people with whom we feel most comfortable. It also determines if we feel part of the country and community in which we live or whether we feel that we are outsiders peering into a world to which we do not fully belong. Those who belong to racial and ethnic minorities often feel invisible, as if they have to try ten times harder just to maintain the status quo. Many live in fear of violent attacks just for the supposed crime of being the wrong color or belonging to an "unacceptable" ethnic group.

Our gender is key in understanding the world and our place in it. In many cultures women are perceived as second-class citizens. Women in the United States did not receive the right to vote until 1920, but with the ascension of the #MeToo and Time's Up movements, equality for women may be within grasp in some countries, but still a long way off in others where a woman's destiny is determined by her father's, brothers' and husband's whims. This brings us to the importance of geographic location. Where one is born determines to a large extent how we perceive reality. As a young child, we are not even that aware of other countries and the various ways life might be different there. We grow up accepting that what we are taught and where we live is the true reality with scant awareness of the vast possibility of life in various cultures throughout the world. In large countries such as the United States, one's view of reality may be dependent upon the region of the country in which one lives. As a Midwestern child in the fifties, I was told that many of the people who lived on the East Coast were socialist and had loose morals, which instilled in me a curiosity and an enticement to go there, but for others, a fear of this alien place.

Class is one of the determining factors in not only affecting the lens through which reality is perceived, but also how one feels about oneself. There may be a sense of being less than if one is from a working or impoverished class; conversely many who are born into wealth view themselves as better than others even though the fact that one's parents might have money has nothing to do with the character of a person. One's intellectual, musical, athletic or artistic gifts, or lack thereof, add an important dimension as to the lens through which one understands the world. A musician hears the tones and vibration of sound in ways that one who is tone deaf does not. An artist may focus on the light, beauty and color of a particular setting; whereas a builder might see the possibility of developing the land. We have the tendency to believe that all see the world as we do, not considering the variations in perspective.

One's religious upbringing, or lack thereof, may be a major influence in determining one's perception of reality. Many of the major religions assert that their beliefs as to the nature of God, how the world was created and the manner in which one should live one's life is the only true reality, the only truth. These assertions have been the justification for war, prejudice and the outright persecution, torture and death of those who held different views. Religious indoctrination that seeks to instill self-hate and obedience in its followers is, at times, so extreme that a person may display the PTSD symptoms of one who has been brainwashed or been in a cult. The lack of tolerance and acceptance of others' spiritual beliefs has been one of the dark marks on the world. This intolerance defies the teaching of the great religious figures of the last 3,000 years, making a mockery of the teachings of love, acceptance and compassion for all.

One might be reading this list of defining factors and respond to them differently depending on one's age and generation. Young women often to do not understand how hard older women worked to alter gender inequality, a struggle that goes back centuries. The freedom to pursue one's innate sexual identity was not even an option a generation ago. Rather it was something that needed to be hidden and for which one felt great shame. Many died violent deaths to achieve self-determination in whom one can love. For centuries, there was prohibition for those of different racial groups marrying. In many countries, this prohibition has been lifted with a new mixed race emerging. Soon more will check "other" more than any other classification on the census form. For some these changes have been met with a violent pushback as demonstrated by the whiplash in the United States with the election of the first African-American president followed by one that supports White Supremacist views and the deportation of many non-whites from the country.

The significance of the energetic imprint of the land cannot be overstated. The land holds the vibration of all who came before for good or ill. Many make pilgrimages to sacred sites throughout the world that hold a vibration of peace and expansion of the heart. Others avoid locations where violence and torture dominate the energetic vibration of the land. There are countries in which the genocide and enslavement of some of its citizens house a negative vibration that spawns further violence.

The cultural lens through which we view reality is composed of myriad cognitive and energetic influences that is further enhanced by one's ancestral and karmic imprints. If we are aware of the power of these imprints to shape our perceptions of reality, then we can be free to listen to the voice within to determine what we truly believe and what type of life will bring the greatest joy and meaning to our lives. We will then be free to view ourselves and others from a place of compassion and equanimity as we strive to be our best selves and live with kindness and understanding.

Chapter 10

Finding the Culture Within

When I was a child, I saw spirits. When I was seven, we moved to an old Victorian house in which the previous occupant had died. I was terrified of the presence of spirits in the house and received numerous spankings for screaming when I saw these spirits and for "telling lies" about seeing something that was not there. When I went into the Peace Corps and lived in Malaysian Borneo, ghosts abounded and everyone saw them. There was one ghost named Pontianak that was a beautiful young woman with long dark hair and pale skin that would seduce men and then suck the life force out of them. At the time I was 22 years old with long dark hair and pale skin. I was told that I could never leave the house alone at night as someone might believe that I was Pontianak and try to kill me. I asked if it were not possible to tell the difference between a ghost and a person. I was told that they both look equally real.

It was in this moment that I realized the ways in which one perceives reality is much greater than whether one eats with chopsticks, silverware or with her hands, but extends literally to what one is able to sense and comprehend. One day I was starting to bathe at the communal bathing platform. From out of nowhere, a young man appeared with a machete and sliced the head off a poisonous snake that was about to attack me. I had no awareness that the snake was near and that I was in harm's way. The capacity of the people in the village of Matu to recognize the subtle messages from the natural world never failed to amaze me. Although they did not have the academic training that I had, their ability to perceive a coming storm or tidal surge, the clues in nature as to when to plant and when to harvest or the threat of attack from a python, crocodile or poisonous snake compelled me to understand that there were other forms of intelligence that far surpassed my abilities. The things that we are able to see and comprehend are different from culture to culture depending on what is necessary to survive.

One of my students became quite ill and was not getting better despite the best effort of the local shamans. I accompanied this student and her mother on the two-day boat ride to a hospital in the nearest town. Neither of them had ever ventured this far from their village. As soon as we arrived, I literally had to push the two of them into a taxi to take them to the hospital. Their terrified eyes spoke volumes as we slowly made our way to the hospital over bumpy roads in a strange box on wheels. Neither of them had ever seen cars or buses let alone a road. After my student was safely admitted to the hospital and I had translated to the mother that she was not allowed to stay with her, I attempted to get the mother on a bus to go to the home of a fellow Peace Corps volunteer where we could stay until her daughter was better. The mother was terrified of entering the bus; she sat down on the steps to the bus and sobbed, blocking the way for anyone to get on or off the bus. The irate bus driver screamed at us in Chinese to move, which only served to intensify the sobs. After twenty minutes, I was able to get her on her feet. We then walked the five miles to my friend's house in 100-degree heat, lugging our bags with us. As we struggled along in the heat, I berated myself for not having thought to better prepare them for the prospect of seeing large moving vehicles. In my cultural ignorance, it had not occurred to me that they had never seen a car or a bus.

In the fifty years from when I first arrived until the present day, the people of Matu have gone through mind-boggling changes. As previously noted, the women were bare breasted and now they are covered from head to toe in traditional Islamic dress. They have gone from being largely unaware of the larger world to having televisions, the Internet and the ability to travel by car, bus and plane, whereas in the past the only means of travel was by boat. Electricity and indoor plumbing are now available for all, although some feel that relieving oneself in a special room in the house is unclean and smelly. Today most women are married in two different wedding gowns with two different services, the traditional dress of the past and a white Western wedding dress. My friends there have gone from living in huts with grass thatched roofs to homes with all of the modern amenities. Before only a few lucky children were allowed the opportunity for even a 6th grade education, to the present time in which many have college and even graduate school educations. The early primary grades had been taught by teachers whose education only extended to the fourth grade; most of the government leaders could not read or write, now they have masters and doctoral degrees.

I ponder how the psyche adapts to these rapid changes in reality as the old ways of perceiving existence is supplanted by a patched-together blend of traditional Islamic thought, a global Western consciousness, and the rituals and traditions of their indigenous culture. As I journeyed to my guides to better understand this query, I was told that the mind is very flexible and resilient. As long as the mind stays open and fluid, then the energy that surrounds various beliefs moves and shifts like the wind, blowing away an old perspective for a new one. The difficulty arises when a given belief becomes so entrenched that it becomes a solidified thought form or block. When a belief is fixed, then it is next to impossible to shift the energy around it. The beliefs are like spikes that hold the tent in place; only a powerful wind can blow the tent down, releasing the energy attached to the beliefs. Conversely, the beliefs might change, but if the energy attached to the beliefs is not healed and transformed, the energy will call in beliefs that match the vibration of the old beliefs.

As many developing nations are similarly swept up in the rush to modernity, will the ability to perceive, interact and connect to the spirit world and the ability to see beyond a subtle veil be lost? Or will this ability be shared with those in the West in order that a rich blend of what is best in all cultures may be preserved? One of the greatest gifts in my life has been not only the ability to live in a radically different culture with its different beliefs and customs, but most importantly the invitation to be initiated into an ancient healing practice in which I was taught how to interface with the spirit world and to work with the energetic realms to heal and transform people's lives. As a psychologist trained in the West, I had been taught to help those who had suffered severe harm, trauma and neglect through traditional talk therapy. When I blended my Western training with what I learned from a gifted indigenous healer in Borneo regarding the energetic nature of our being, miraculous transformations resulted.

The Melting Pot

With the advent of the Internet and the ability to travel to, and in some instances move to, far-off parts of the world, many of the ancient rituals and traditions are fading away to be replaced by an amalgam of cultural traditions. Many are deciding to create their own unique ceremonies for the three major events in most of our lives—birth, marriage and the rituals for the dead and dying. Some embrace the sense of liberation that arises from the blending of culture, ethnicity and the freedom to love whomever one chooses. Others resist these changes and cling to old traditions, beliefs and customs. It is as if the tribal identity that reflected back who one is and where one belongs has been shattered like a broken mirror with distorted images of people who look and dress differently staring back from the various glass fragments; one's sense of coherent reality smashed.

Wars are fought over the global surge to modernity and who has the right to determine another's reality and resources. Cultural wars ensue in developed countries as to who is welcome from developing countries. There is a sense of instability throughout the world as many seek to find a foundation, a reality in which to ground oneself.

Why is it that some embrace a global consciousness and a blending of cultures whereas others fight it, longing to stay with what is known? There are a number of factors to consider in grasping a better understanding of this quandary. The teachings from our families and ancestors coupled with the energy attached to these beliefs can be a key element. Some take great pride in their ancestral lineage and stress the importance of keeping this line pure. Others grow up in a family that teaches inclusivity, often supported by religious or spiritual beliefs that assert that we are all created equal and all should be treated with love and respect. And yet, within families there can be considerable disagreement on the subject. Faint traces from other lifetimes can influence whether we welcome in someone from a particular culture or country. If, as a woman, one had a lifetime of abuse, oppression and suffering at the hands of one's father and husband, she may have a genuine fear of men from this culture and not be clear why. Conversely, we may have had lifetimes in a particular area of the world that were peaceful and happy, and open-heartedly embrace people from these countries.

Vibrations of the Land

The energetic vibration of the land strongly influences how the people who live upon it perceive and experience reality. Everything has an energetic vibration. The density of the earth holds the vibration of significant occurrences for eons if it is not healed or altered in some way. People travel to destinations that are believed to hold healing or sacred energy, and they avoid places that hold negative ones. Land that has been ravaged for development, mining and drilling often carries the energy of a bombed target. Land where wars have been waged hold the violence and trauma of war, death and destruction. Fortunately, the negative vibration of a traumatized place can be healed and transformed, similar to the healing of a person's energetic body after a traumatic event. The key to this healing and transformation lies in a cognitive awareness of the extent of the trauma and the desire for it to be transformed.

A few months after 9/11, I went with my son to the site where the World Trade Center once stood. I had braced myself to feel the vibration of terror, horror and death. Instead I found a golden hue that represented the love and healing energy that many people from around the world sent to the area. Many people who are shamanic practitioners worked tirelessly to heal the souls of those who died or lost part of their soul essence there. In doing so, light columns were placed at the site to heal and transform the souls who remained behind and for the land itself. Although I believe in the power of this work to heal and transform, I was ecstatic to experience the lightness of the area after such a devastating tragedy, and to experience that love was able to heal such a violent and hateful act.

A key element in any transformative healing is to bring a conscious intent to the task. The American people were united in their support of all impacted by 9/11 and poured love and prayers into the area, shifting the vibration of the horror there. After World War II, the German people had to contend with the collective shame and remorse that they had allowed their government to torture and exterminate six million Jewish people and those who were gay and lesbian. Hitler had designated and exterminated other groups he viewed as unacceptable such as the Gypsies. An additional estimated 100 million people died throughout the world as a result of the war that Hitler began. After the war, the German people went through a period of soul searching to determine how these incredible atrocities were allowed to occur. They took responsibility for having turned a blind eye to the roundup and torture of Jews, gays and others deemed less than human, for following a man who had anointed them as the chosen people destined to rule the world, and for believing in their superiority. As a result, Germany is now a leader of freedom, innovation and economic success throughout the world. The conscious desire to atone for what had been perpetrated in their name helped to heal the vibration of the land. Without this, the vibration of the land would have held the horror of the inhumanity that had been committed.

Westerners that colonialized the land now known as South Africa instigated an inhumane policy of Apartheid in which the native people were segregated with few rights and no say in how they were governed. Many atrocities were committed until world economic pressure forced open elections that heralded in the Presidency of Nelson Mandela. Mandela had spent 27 years in prison for being a voice in the opposition to the Apartheid regime. Instead of seeking revenge and retribution for the harm done to his people thereby creating more death and destruction, he stressed the importance of healing the wrongs that had been done through the Truth and Reconciliation Commission. Mandela emphasized the importance of understanding and forgiveness rather than further violence. In doing so he helped to heal the harm that had been done, and became a major voice for peace and justice throughout the world. Mandela won the Nobel Peace Prize in 1993 along with former President Frederik Willem de Klerk for their work in the peaceful termination of the Apartheid regime. Again, by bringing to consciousness the suffering and harm that was done to the native African people, a healing for the nation and for the land ensued. According to the BBC, South Africa has more murders per capita than any other country in the world, indicating that there is still more work to be done to heal the violent imprint from years of oppression of the majority of the people living there. It also signifies the need for individual healing of its most traumatized citizens.

For centuries, North America was home to a collection of

various tribes of people that held the utmost respect for the land, the elements and the teachings from their power animals and spirit guides. When Europeans arrived to stake a claim to this vast, magnificent continent, they committed genocide to establish their claim to the land, justifying this seizure by defining the people as savages. They then kidnapped people from the African continent and made them slaves, ordering them to do the hard work of clearing and developing this vast land. Although there has been minor lip service to the harm that was done to both the Native American and African people brought to this country, the energetic imprint of the violence done to two races of people remains.

The actions of those who founded this great country were based on the desire for self-determination, freedom and equality for all, but the underlying assumption of the superiority of the white male blinded them to the inhumanity of their actions. Implied in this stance is that they had the right to do whatever they wanted to do to create the country of their dreams. The inability of the American government to begin a dialogue on the misguided beliefs of this time in history has resulted in an insidious racist thread that lives not only in the hearts and minds of some of the populace, but also in the land. With the election of the first African-American president, the racist thread spawned reaction that led to a president that espouses White Supremacist views in the subsequent presidency.

The energetic imprint of this violence and the underlying belief that the United States has the right to do whatever it wants to globally benefit its own agenda has created a country with violent predilections. The United States has one of the largest militaries in the world, and again according to the BBC, the highest crime rate per capita as well as the greatest number of people imprisoned, with the non-white population comprising a disproportionately high percentage of the incarcerations. The United States also has the highest rate of gun ownership per capita than any other country in the world. This is not to imply that the United States is not a great country with many wonderful and amazing people who are kind and caring; it merely suggests that the imprint of violence and racism is present in the origins of the country, and that the energy of this permeates the land influencing beliefs that flow from this energy.

There are many beautiful and talented people who work tirelessly to heal and transform the negative imprint of the land, but until there is a collective acknowledgement of the harm done to others in the creation of the country, it cannot be fully healed. The historical narrative of the origin of the United States stresses the valor and brilliance of the colonials to free themselves from British rule, but omits the genocide of the Native Americans and the destruction of their way of life. Until the latter is acknowledged, the energy of the horror of genocide will permeate the land as beliefs hold the energy in place.

In beginning such a dialogue, there is no need for blame or defensiveness. It is important to take into consideration the beliefs and customs of the time. Women were not seen as equal citizens, could not vote and had no say in how the country was founded beyond subtle influences women might have had on their husbands. It was also a period in history in which European countries believed it was their right to colonialize underdeveloped countries and vied to see whose flag flew in the most places. The underlying racist imprint of white colonialism cannot be healed and transformed until it is squarely acknowledged and addressed. Sadly, all too often politicians use the fear of the other as a tool to control and manipulate its citizenry to benefit the few. Many prefer to vote against their economic self-interest rather than align themselves with cultural or racial minorities who share hardships similar to their own.

Fear

From the time of the cavemen, mankind has feared the unknown and has lived within tribal communities for support and protection. The fear of the unknown and the possibility of an external threat lies deep within our karmic awareness. We all have a flight/fight response hardwired into our physiology to alert us to an attack or of impending danger. There are many instances in which fear is our ally, but all too often it is debilitating and harmful to the smooth flow of our energy and to our well-being.

The fear of something or someone can be passed from one family member to the next, whether it is the fear of another race of people or of something rather insignificant. For years I had an irrational fear of dead mice and passed this fear onto my son. I would behave like a silly person, hiding and screaming when our cat brought us a "gift". I would beg him to pick up the dead mouse and dispose of it when he was just a small boy. In my hysteria my son absorbed the terror that I felt and it became part of his energy field. As I became more comfortable with dead things, this fear vanished; although I never relish the task of cleaning up dead mice, I do it without any fanfare. The fear of mice lived in my strong athletic son years after I was free of this fear, teaching me the power of a negative energetic imprint to be passed from one generation to the next on something as insignificant as dead mice. Just imagine what can be taught and transmitted when the issue is of greater significance.

All too often, humans are taught to fear and hate another. As a child, I was captivated by the Rodgers and Hammerstein song in *South Pacific*, *You've Got to Be Carefully Taught*:

You've got to be taught to hate and fear
You've got to be taught from year to year
It's got to be drummed in your dear little ear
You've got to be carefully taught.

You've got to be taught to be afraid
Of people whose eyes are oddly made

And people whose skin is a different shade
You've got to be carefully taught.

You've got to be taught before it's too late
Before you are six or seven or eight
To hate all the people your relatives hate
You've got to be carefully taught.

Of the many songs of my childhood, this one comes floating into my consciousness whenever I hear a politician extolling us to hate the enemy of his choosing. If they repeat again and again that a certain ethnic or racial group is evil, will harm us and that they hate us, we are being primed to follow this politician into war or outright aggression towards anyone of this ethnic or racial group. Some politicians have the ability to unite people around a common goal that benefits all, but all too often, politicians attempt to unite us around a common foe from which, according to them, only they can protect us. We are urged, through the exploitation of an innate fear of the other that may arise from both a karmic and ancestral imprint, to abandon our longing for peace and understanding.

If we know someone that is different from us that we truly like, we can begin to overcome the programmed tendency to fear or hate the other. Many of us were taught that being gay was seen as shameful, a crime against nature. There was an irrational fear that if one associated with "those people" that their tendency might rub off on us. Many who preferred the love of someone of the same gender led tortured lives denying who they were, hiding their true heart, and in too many cases, ending their own lives as the pain was too great to bear. Yet, as more and more brave souls came out of the closet, forcing their families to realize that their beloved son, daughter, niece or nephew were gay, and that they were the same loveable being that they had always been, people's attitudes began to shift. As a result of a shift in attitude as to what one had been taught about the immorality of homosexuality, individual states began to legalize the right to marry someone of the same gender and to end discrimination towards gays and lesbians. In 2015, the US Supreme Court legalized same-sex marriage in all 50 states, overthrowing the legitimacy of what many had been carefully taught to hate and fear.

This same realization arises when one knows and likes someone of a different ethnic or racial group. When I was in the Peace Corps, the people in the village to which I was assigned were practicing Muslims. They were the kindest, most open-hearted and accepting people that I had ever met. When my government began to portray the Muslim people as terrorists and our enemy, it was in clear contradiction to my felt experience of the peaceful nature of the Muslim people that I know. Yes, there are Muslims that are terrorists just as there are white people that are terrorists. When Timothy McVeigh blew up the Alfred P. Murrah Federal Building in Oklahoma City in 1995, not all white men were condemned as domestic terrorists. When a white person commits mass murder, it is deemed the act of a single deranged individual. When a person of color commits mass murder, it is considered to be the orchestrated act of terrorism. We must constantly be mindful that when we are frightened by a horrific mass murder, that the fear we feel is not then manipulated into hating or fearing an entire group of people. This type of manipulation can be used to justify the expansion of the military, the curbing of individual freedoms and the urging of citizens to support unjustified wars.

Most who perpetrate acts of violence do so as an expression of the pain that they are in. Perhaps the energy of growing up in a violent household, surviving the horror of war or the terror of gang violence is alive in one's energy body, sitting there waiting for the right moment, for what is erroneously believed to be a cathartic release, through the expulsion of this violent energy in the most horrifying way possible.

In the dualist thinking of right and wrong, good or bad, we do not consider the complexities that make each of us who we are as we contend with the trace energies of previous lifetimes, the beliefs and energies that are absorbed from our families and culture. If a child is demeaned and belittled at home, the energy of this cruelty is in the energy body as well as the belief that, "I am no good." All too often this child is the one who is bullied or is the one who bullies. My very first job, after receiving a master's degree in school psychology, was as a therapist for nine elementary schools. The majority of the children that I worked with were either the bully or the one who was bullied. As I got to know these little guys and their backgrounds, they came from the type of home in which they were constantly degraded and made to feel unworthy, as if something was wrong with them. Some overcompensated by becoming the braggart and the tormenter, all the while feeling less than, whereas others walked around with an invisible "kick me" sign plastered to their energy field. Their pain was the same as the suffering in their homes; it merely manifested differently.

If these children and their families do not receive help and healing, they continue to live trapped in these painful imprints. The bullies marry the victims, the dance of domestic abuse repeated from one generation to the next. Often the bullies and the braggarts ascend the ladder of success, striving for external validation as they become the bosses from hell, the gang leaders or the politicians that spew hate and intolerance for anyone who disagrees with them. All too often those who are bullied live half-lives frequently numbing their pain through an array of addictive behaviors and they become the fodder for the abusers. This repeating pattern occurs within families, communities, the workplace, the nation and between nation states. It is a dynamic that can be healed and altered if we allow ourselves to open to the energetic power of our true nature. In doing so, we can lessen the energetic and cognitive power of what we were taught to shape who we are and how we perceive reality.

Often there is a tendency to judge and fear those who are in great pain and act in ways that are harmful to themselves and others. Some describe them as bad, evil or as losers. Unless one lives in a culture or family that encourages compassion and understanding, there is a cultural or ancestral bias that encourages one to see a person in pain as the other, distancing ourselves from their pain and denying their humanity. We tend not to consider the ways in which we are alike or the shared pain that might lie between us. I suggest that we consider a both/and approach. I am in no way advocating that we ignore or dismiss a person's bad actions; people need to be held accountable for their behavior. But if we lose sight of the humanity within them, we also lose touch with an aspect of our own humanity. When a boss bullies, belittles and constantly criticizes us, we can cower in fear or we can diminish the power they have over us, by seeing their pain and woundedness. If a person feels good about himself, there is no need to bully. Recognizing our boss's pain and vulnerability, we can respond in a kind rather than fearful manner, thereby shifting the energetic dynamic between us. If we are able to perceive the pain and harm that has been done to the bully and bullied, our compassionate heart opens to them. When we are kind to another, it shifts the energy between us— not from a place of weakness, but from a place of strength. It takes strength to see the beauty in another even when they are acting badly.

There are many energies that each of us carries that mask our true hearts. If we are screamed at in anger, this angry scream lives in our energy field, waiting for a trigger that will ignite the scream and send it hurling towards another. The scream is not who we truly are nor is it who the other truly is; it is merely the energy that we have absorbed, waiting for release. My next book will focus on ways to recognize and heal negative emotional states and energies. Within each of us is a kind, compassionate soul. It is much more important to grow our compassion than our fear.

War and Peace

There are many things that we believe to be true or as part of our essential nature that may not be true at all. We may carry the imprint karmically, ancestrally and culturally of some beliefs that we accept as true, but in fact might be the relics of an evolutionary process. We are at a key moment in the evolution of man as we move from a tribal consciousness to a global one. Much of the instability that people feel personally and globally rests in the turbulence of this time in history. It may be helpful to pause and examine our assumptions, to discern if they are truths or merely notions that we have absorbed from our families and our society.

It has long been considered that it is man's basic nature to seek war as a way of settling disputes and disagreements. It is such a part of the lexicon that we use the language of war in healing illness: we wage war on cancer, we fight death to the bitter end, or describe the one who died as a warrior to the end. My family often joked that I had been born a pacifist. I was born a month before the end of World War II. The family lore is that I screamed each night until the war was over and then slept peacefully through the night from that point on. Perhaps this is an aspect of my karmic imprint, as I have always felt that war is a barbaric way of resolving disagreements. I have registered my disquiet with war by marching in the streets to protest my country's propensity to engage in one war after another. Each of us carries within us karmic traces of lifetimes when we lived in peace, and lifetimes in which our lives were altered or ruined by the futility of war.

My biases towards peace stated, I would like us to consider that war is not inherent in our nature, but the tendency to go into battle is part of our karmic, ancestral and cultural imprints. Wars have been part of recorded history going back to the advent of patriarchy. Those who are fans of *Game of Thrones* and other medieval sagas observe up close the brutality of hand-to-hand combat and the lack of morality in observing honorable rules of engagement. If one side has a much larger, better-trained and equipped army, then the other side resorts to trickery and sneak attacks to level the playing field, not unlike modern warfare when terrorism is used to counter large military might.

The trauma of war has been widely documented with soldiers suffering from soul-shattering PTSD from the stress of needing to kill the enemy before one is killed. The energy of war does not stay on the battlefield, but comes home with the soldier spreading like a virus to loved ones and friends. The energy of war is insidious as it flows into the energy body and consciousness of the warrior, as part of the soul essence leaves from the horror of what lay before him. Many returning soldiers forget where they are as they are pulled into a dissociated memory of threat and violence, sometimes attacking those they love as the energy of the battle flows through their being, eradicating the safety and reality of where they are and who they are with at the moment. Their families absorb the terror of battle as it becomes part of their energy field as well. Children act out this terror in their play and at times on one another; the imprint of war is instilled in the next generation's consciousness and energy field.

There are families in which serving in the military is part of the family culture. It is the patriotic thing to do, the right thing to do. Often it defines what it means to be a man by being a warrior. It is part of the ancestral lineage. But most importantly, it is the cultural message about war. Those in power need an army to defend their interests. They need to convince their subjects that their cause is a just one, worthy of defending their King, leader or president at the cost of sacrificing their own lives for his continued reign. One is deemed unpatriotic, a traitor, if they do not follow their leader into battle. Centuries ago the leader actually led his people into battle. Now they bunker down in indestructible locations, safe from harm.

Currently there is enough nuclear power and conventional weaponry to blow up the planet several times over. Perhaps it is time to contemplate if it is truly in our nature and in our basic self-interest to use war as a way of solving disputes. As we evolve into a global community, it may be time to consider that we are all on the same side. It is important to be cognizant that there are a few extremely wealthy individuals who are striving to rule the world through economic dominance who urge us to fight with one another so we will not notice what they are doing.

Awakening to Our True Essence

As we consider all of the influences that conspire to create our reality, take a moment to pause to listen to our inner voice. To do this we must first quiet our mind. This can be achieved by walking in nature, meditating or sitting still while looking out over a beautiful vista. We are all very easily distracted by the many details of life and the constant bombardment of the media, be it TV, live streaming, social media or video games. All of these endeavors distract us from listening to ourselves while creating a vulnerability to be manipulated or programmed by external forces. I am not advocating that one should stop utilizing these methods of connecting to the world and to play, but rather to be mindful of the influence they have on what we think and believe.

I discovered in my twenties that there were two voices in my mind. There was a voice that was filled with all the "shoulds" that I was carefully taught which included everything from what I should wear to what I should do for a living, and what I should think and feel in a given situation. The other voice carried what I truly thought and felt. I had been taught/encouraged to ignore the latter voice, especially when it was directly in opposition to all of those "shoulds". Allow yourself to notice if there are competing voices in your head. If so, allow yourself to be with them both in order to discern which arises from your true heart and which stems from what you have been taught to think and feel in a given situation. Listen to the first thought that arises when making a decision. Does this voice tell you how you really feel, or is it the automatic response that you have been taught to have? Listen to your dreams at night. Are they revealing what you are processing on an unconscious level that may not have risen to conscious awareness?

As a child, in a moment of anger, many of us promised ourselves that we would never say to our children what our parents just said to us; yet with no conscious thought, these words come streaming out of our mouths with an inner gasp that laments that we sound just like our parents. Acknowledge the power of these imprints to still be with us. The first step in changing them is the awareness that they are there. Once we realize that these beliefs, prejudices and harsh words do not truly represent who we are or what we feel, they lose their energetic power and can float away.

Take time to pay attention to your daydreams and fantasies as within them are glimpses of what our hearts long for, what we want to manifest in our lives. If these fantasies are angry or vengeful, ask yourself from whence they arise. Is this how you truly feel and what you truly want to do or is this what you were taught to do in a given situation? Were you taught to always stand up for yourself, to fight back if anyone tried to take advantage of you, and that you were a sissy if you did not? Is this angry energy in your field your own anger, or does it belong to someone else? If we were yelled at as a child, this anger may remain in our field and be activated in a similar situation to that in which we were initially demeaned. If the anger is our own, take a moment to consider if this is an old wound or hurt. One might commit a minor transgression, but it carries the vibration of an earlier, more significant injury. The pain evoked from a minor slight might be all out of proportion to what is triggered by an old unresolved trauma. Many relationships are ended by one person feeling as if they are not being listened to and taken seriously, while the second person feels that the other is making a big deal out of nothing. Both are usually true and both realities need to be considered. There needs to be space in the relationship to explore why the hurt was so big and from whence this pain originated, just as the other person's perspective that this is an overreaction needs to be considered. Some grow up in families in which very little is considered worthy of becoming upset and disconcerted; after all, things do not always run smoothly and as one might like them. If we immediately fall into a defensive, "I'm right, you're wrong" stance, the relationship can be in jeopardy. Rather, if, with love, there is space to hear the upset, understand the initial wound, then a deeper level of intimacy can ensue.

We are energetic beings. We are impacted both vibrationally and cognitively by our families, our culture and what we have learned and experienced in previous incarnations. With the advent of the Internet, a global consciousness and the steady stream of information hurtling toward us, we have the opportunity to truly discern our own truth if we listen carefully to our reactions and feelings to what is before us. If, however, we lack awareness of the power of all of this information to interface with the energetic vibrations that often mask our true essence, we can be manipulated to perceive the world in ways that benefit the few and are harmful to us.

I noticed while in the woods, staring at the natural scene in front of me, that one insect ate another. Then it dawned upon me that every creature eats another. As I journeyed on this, I both saw and was told that the earth and all of the beings on the earth, including the plants, trees, rocks and bodies of water, are different vibrations of the same whole. When we eat, we are merging with the vibration of the food we are eating and should welcome and thank this vibration for merging with us. When we intentionally harm another, we also harm ourselves; a part of our soul essence is lost and damaged just as the other's is through our actions. My guides then shared the words to a song.

Spirit come, bring us peace,
Help us live as one
Help us know that we're all the same
And in our hearts are one.

Glossary of Terms

The following terms are quite complex and are open to myriad interpretation. Thus they are not to be taken as the precise definition of these terms but rather as a roadmap to understanding what I am trying to convey in the book.

Alters is the term given to distinct personalities that reside within the ego structure of one who has Multiple Personalities or who has been diagnosed with Dissociative Identity Disorder.

Buddhist Mind. In Tibetan Buddhism the mind resides in the heart and one thinks with the heart. Westerners tend to think of the mind residing in the head near the brain.

The Chakra System is an ancient metaphysical system originating in India, which ties the complexities of the universe to the intricacies of the human existence. There are seven major chakras, 40 secondary ones, and, according to traditional writings, 88,000 in all, which leaves scarcely a point on the body that is not open for the reception, transformation, or transferal of energy.

The Dreambody operates on various frequency bands. When an unconscious memory surfaces to consciousness, it alters the frequency band of the psyche. The dreambody is holographic in nature, moving in and out of the physical body, capable of functions beyond those we in the West believe possible.

Energetic Imprints are energetic vibrations that live in our energy body that are absorbed from our families and ancestors as well as from previous incarnations and from the culture and community in which we live.

Extraction is the removal of energy that does not belong in the body or the energy field. This unwanted energy enters when there is soul loss and causes physical or emotional illness. It needs to be removed before lost parts of the soul can be returned. Spirit guides or power animals remove the unwanted energy by working through a healer who is physically doing the extraction.

Holographic refers to the ability of energy to materialize and de-materialize, to move in and out of matter, and to travel on its own and then re-materialize and reconnect with matter as needed. Scientists now believe a phenomenon such as *Star Wars'* Princess Leia's ghostly image emerging through a light beam from R2-D2 is more fact than fiction.

Introjects are aspects of psychic energy from one person being taken into the psychic structure of another. A parent's fear and anxiety may be absorbed and taken into the psychic structure of the child along with the belief that a certain activity or person is dangerous.

Multiple Personality refers to a condition when there are two or more distinct personalities residing within the same body and psychic structure, and are usually discernable as being uniquely different. Often these personalities do not have awareness that the other exists and each may have activities and friends that only they know and visit. This condition arises from extreme and often repeated trauma at an early age and is considered to be an adaptive way for the psyche to endure such trauma and continue to function. Currently it is believed that there is a Dissociative Continuum with distinct personalities being at one end, and brief periods of disruption in normal functions of memory, consciousness, and identity at the other end. For instance, if a woman witnesses a horrible car crash, she may not be able to remember that she was even there let alone what transpired. Each time that she sees a car accident, she may go into a Dissociative state and not be present, but the rest of the time she functions normally.

Non-ordinary Reality is considered to be a realm that we cannot concretely see but in which we can learn to travel and know through going into a trance state. Traditional cultures refer to this reality as dreamtime or the other time. Power animals live in the lower realms of non-ordinary reality whereas spirit guides inhabit the upper realms. Intuitive wisdom originates in non-ordinary reality.

Ordinary Reality is the concrete reality in which we can see, smell, and touch things. In some traditions it is referred to as the middle realm. When one becomes proficient in shamanic journeying, it is possible to travel forward and backward in ordinary reality. Most of us spend the majority of our time in ordinary reality.

Power Animals are guides and teachers that inhabit the lower realms of non-ordinary reality. These animals exist on a vibrational frequency and bring us the teachings or medicine that we need. Some are with us our entire life while others come to us for a specific teaching or task. Most of us have an intuitive sense of which animals we are most connected to and who our power animals might be.

Programming is a process in which the beliefs and words of one person or group are placed within the psychic structure of another through torture and/or hypnosis.

Projections are unintegrated aspects of the psyche that are energetically sent to another. If a woman unconsciously feels that she is not bright and capable of being successful, she may project onto others that they feel she is stupid even if they do not, or conversely she may believe that they are stupid or inadequate and send this energetic belief to them. If one of the people to whom this projection was made feels inadequate, then she will take in the projection as truth. This is called projective identification and is when one person feels the energy of the projection, takes in this energy, and believes it to be true. See Chapter 7 for a deeper explanation.

Psychopomp is a shamanic practice in which the shaman, through shamanic journeying, accompanies the soul of the recently deceased to the other side and does healing work on the other side for the dead.

Ritual Abuse is when a person is harmed, tortured or abused repeatedly, and the abuse has the same pattern or ritual accompanying it each time the torture occurs.

Sadomasochism is a practice or tendency in which one person plays the role of perpetrator and the other of the victim.

A Shaman is a healer who has the ability to travel to other realms of reality, communicate and work with spirit guides and power animals to bring about healing for individuals, the community at large, and the earth and all that inhabit the earth.

Shamanism is an ancient healing method dating back at least 60,000 years that has been practiced in almost every culture throughout the world. It involves working with guides and teachers from non-ordinary reality to bring about healing, and to gather information and wisdom from other realms of knowledge.

A Shamanic Journey is the process of going into a trance state via percussive sound, hallucinogenic plants, or a meditative state to communicate with guides and teachers in non-ordinary reality. A skilled shaman can walk in both ordinary and non-ordinary reality simultaneously.

Shape-shifting is when a person or animal merges with another form of energy and shifts into that being. Often this is done energetically rather than materially.

The Soul carries an awareness of our purpose and place in the universe. Within the soul are the psyche, energy, and physical bodies that are vibrationally housed in the dreambody.

Soul Loss is when part of the soul or essence splits away from the core and is vibrationally disconnected from the core aspect of the person. Soul loss occurs through traumatic occurrences or through the disconnection of the soul to the spiritual realm and to the presence of spirit in everything.

Soul Retrieval is when a shaman travels into the dreambody of a person with soul loss and finds the split-off part of the soul, does a healing for the soul part, and returns it to the core vibrational frequency of the person.

Spirit Guides are our teachers that live in the upper realm of non-ordinary reality and provide guidance and teaching. Some of these guides are dear friends who have crossed over and who have come to help us on the physical plane. Others may be teachers or loved ones from other lifetimes, while some may be mythic beings who embody the divine energy and wisdom of the universe.

A Spiritual Warrior is a person who is comfortable traveling in non-ordinary reality and in working with negative as well as positive energies in both ordinary and non-ordinary reality.

Tonglen is a Tibetan Buddhist practice in which one breathes in the suffering of another on the in breath and sends out love and compassion to the other on the out breath thereby transforming the suffering through taking it into oneself.

Trance is an altered state of consciousness when one can see beyond the veils of ordinary reality into other realms of existence, and communicate with guides and teachers in these realms.

Vibrational Frequency is our energetic mode of operation. Our bodies are slowed down energetic frequencies that have become matter. When we travel to other realms of reality through entering a trance state, we increase or raise our vibrational frequency. The more we journey or enter trance, the further we can travel, bringing us access to greater information and wisdom.

Endnotes

1. Arnold Mindell, *Dreambody: The Body's Role in Revealing the Self* (Boston, MA: Sigo Press, 1982).

2. Shalila Sharamon and Bodo J. Baginski, *The Chakra-Handbook* (Wilmot, WI: Lotus Light Publications/Shangri-La, 1988).

3. For more information on Tenzin Wangyal Rinpoche, his teachings, books and retreat center, go to <www.ligmincha.org>.

4. Rhonda Byrne, *The Secret* (Portland, Oregon: Beyond Words Publishing, 2007).

5. For more information on Abraham-Hicks go to their website: <www.Abraham-Hicks.com>.

6. For more information on the chakra system see Anodea Judith, and Ann Drake, *Healing of the Soul: Shamanism and Psyche*, Chapter 7.

7. Eckhart Tolle, *A New Earth: Awakening to Your Life's Purpose* (London: Plume Books, 2006).

8. This philosophy comes from a variety of sources, most notably the entity Michael. There have been numerous books written about the teachings of Michael; see Jose Stevens' books on the entity Michael.

9. First Ladakh and then Sikkim were annexed into India in 1975. China invaded and then annexed Tibet in the 1950s.

10. Marianne Williamson, *A Return to Love: Reflections on the Principles of A Course In Miracles* (New York, NY: HarperCollins, pp. 190–191).

11. It goes without saying that many are raised with praise and a realistic appraisal of gifts and talents. The "helicopter generation" is touted as being the most praised and cherished generation of all time.

12. For more information on this, read Richard Schwartz's work on Internal Family Systems. See his website and list of

publications and trainings at <www.selfleadership.org>.

13. The six directions in some shamanic traditions are East, South, West, North, Above and Below.

14. See Sandra Ingerman, *Soul Retrieval*, and Ann Drake, *Healing of the Soul: Shamanism and Psyche*, for more information on the process of soul retrieval.

15. Ann Drake, *Healing of the Soul: Shamanism and Psyche* (Ithaca, NY: Busca, Inc., 2003).

16. CG Jung, *The Archetypes and the Collective Unconscious* (1959).

17. Shirley Andrews, *Atlantis: Insights from a Lost Civilization* (St. Paul, MN: Llewellyn Publications, 1997).

18. See Jose Stevens' collection of books on the Michael teachings.

Bibliography

Andrews, Shirley. *Atlantis: Insights from a Lost Civilization*. St. Paul, MN: Llewellyn Publications, 1997.

Brennan, Barbara. *Hands of Light*. New York: Bantam Books, 1987.

Byrne, Rhonda. *The Secret*. New York: Atria Books, 2006.

Dickson, MG. *A Sarawak Anthology*. London: University of London Press Ltd., 1965.

Drake, AM. *Healing of the Soul: Shamanism and Psyche*. Ithaca, NY: Busca, Inc., 2003.

Eliade, Mircea. *Shamanism: Archaic Techniques of Ecstasy*. New York: Pantheon, 1964.

Harner, Michael. *The Way of the Shaman*. New York: Harper, 1980.

Ingerman, Sandra. *Soul Retrieval: Mending the Fragmented Self*. New York: HarperCollins, HarperSanFrancisco, 1990.

Judith, Anodea, and Selene Vega. *The Sevenfold Journey: Reclaiming Mind, Body & Spirit Through the Chakras*. Freedom, CA: The Crossing Press, 1993.

Jung, CG. *Modern Man In Search of a Soul*. New York: Harcourt, Brace & World, Inc., 1933.

Mindell, Arnold. *Dreambody: The Body's Role in Revealing the Self*. Boston: Sigo Press, 1982.

Mullen, Vernon. *The Story of Sarawak*. Kuala Lumpur: Oxford University Press, 1967.

Schwartz, Richard C. *Introduction to the Internal Family Systems Model*. Oak Park, IL: Trailheads, 2001.

Sharamon, Shalila, and Bodo J. Baginski. *The Chakra-Handbook*. Wilmot, WI: Lotus Light Publications/Shangri-La, 1988.

Stevens, Jose, and Lena S. Stevens. *Secrets of Shamanism: Tapping the Spirit Power Within You*. New York: Avon, 1988.

Stevens, Jose, and Simon Warwick-Smith. *The Michael Handbook: A Channeled System for Self Understanding*. Sonoma, CA: Warwick Press, 1990.

Talbot, Michael. *The Holographic Universe.* New York: HarperCollins Publishers, 1991.

Tolle, Eckhart. *A New Earth: Awakening to Your Life's Purpose.* London: Plume Books, 2006.

Weiner, Tim. "Senate unit calls US 'most violent' country on earth." *Boston Globe.* March 13, 1991.

Williamson, Marianne. *A Return to Love: Reflections on the Principles of A Course In Miracles.* New York: HarperCollins, 1992 (pp. 190–191).

Winnicott, DW. *The Maturational Process and the Facilitating Environment.* New York: International Universities Press, Inc., 1965.

Wolf, Fred Alan. *The Dreaming Universe.* New York: Touchstone, 1995.

About the Author and Her Work

As a child, Ann saw and sensed spirits but her reporting of such sightings was met with harsh punishment. Gradually she learned to shut down this awareness until it was awakened when she landed in Borneo where the vibrations of the spirit world permeated her entire being. Since the sightings of ghosts and spirits were as commonplace in Borneo as noticing birds and squirrels in the US, it dawned upon Ann that the ability to see these beings from behind the veil is based on whether one believes in their existence. Upon her return to the US in the early seventies, Ann threw herself into the antiwar movement, graduate school and feminism; the awareness of the spirit world squashed by the dominant cultural paradigm and her immersion in creating a more just world.

In the seventies and early eighties, Ann worked in a feminist therapy collective with women who had experienced physical, sexual and emotional trauma. With other like-minded therapists, she strove to define new models of treatment that went beyond the overmedication and long hospitalizations that were common at that time and to bring an awareness of the prevalence of sexual abuse into the mainstream of the collective consciousness.

Faced with treating clients with severe trauma from cult abuse and trauma from incest, rape, and physical and emotional abuse, Ann realized that she needed more training and went back to graduate school to earn a doctorate in clinical psychology at Antioch/New England Graduate School in 1989. Upon graduation Ann was invited to join the faculty and to experience a brief foray into the mainstream of society before returning to Malaysian Borneo to discover her true calling.

Ann was initiated into the Unani tradition of shamanic healing by the Bomoh, a wise and gifted healer. Upon her return, Ann devoted herself to the study and practice of shamanism and has worked towards a clinical and theoretical synthesis of psychology and shamanism. The results of her healing work were so powerful and dramatic that she has presented at various conferences, written numerous articles and a book entitled, *Healing of the Soul: Shamanism and Psyche*, and has offered workshops and trainings for those who are called to be shamanic practitioners. Through a deep immersion into the practice of shamanism, the energetic base of one's being was revealed. Ann began to see and sense the various vibrations that cling to our energy bodies that are not part of one's true nature, but are absorbed from our families, our previous incarnations and the dominant culture. Daily new understandings and insights arise, understandings that Ann wishes to share with the world.

From the Author

Thank you for purchasing *The Energetic Dimension: Understanding Our Karmic, Ancestral and Cultural Imprints*. It is my sincere hope that you found the book stimulating, that it touched your heart and expanded your understanding of how we interact with one another and with society at large. Many of the concepts in the book came from the wisdom of my spirit guides and power animals. It was a true gift and joy to write this book with them. If you have a few moments, please feel free to add your review of the book at your favorite online site for feedback.

My first book, *Healing of the Soul: Shamanism and Psyche*, ISBN-13: 978-1-934934-00-5, is still in print and lays the foundation for many of the concepts in this book.

If you would like more information about my healing work, how to be in touch and to read blog postings or gain information regarding my next book, please visit my website: <http://www.anndrakesoulwork.com>.

My blog postings may also be read on my professional Facebook page: <Ann M Drake, Psy.D>.

BOOKS

O-BOOKS

SPIRITUALITY

O is a symbol of the world, of oneness and unity; this eye
represents knowledge and insight. We publish titles on general
spirituality and living a spiritual life. We aim to inform and help
you on your own journey in this life.
If you have enjoyed this book, why not tell other readers by
posting a review on your preferred book site?

Recent bestsellers from O-Books are:

Heart of Tantric Sex
Diana Richardson
Revealing Eastern secrets of deep love and intimacy to Western
couples.
Paperback: 978-1-90381-637-0 ebook: 978-1-84694-637-0

Crystal Prescriptions
The A-Z guide to over 1,200 symptoms and their healing crystals
Judy Hall
The first in the popular series of six books, this handy little
guide is packed as tight as a pill-bottle with crystal remedies for
ailments.
Paperback: 978-1-90504-740-6 ebook: 978-1-84694-629-5

Take Me To Truth
Undoing the Ego
Nouk Sanchez, Tomas Vieira
The best-selling step-by-step book on shedding the Ego, using the
teachings of *A Course In Miracles*.
Paperback: 978-1-84694-050-7 ebook: 978-1-84694-654-7

The 7 Myths about Love...Actually!
The journey from your HEAD to the HEART of your SOUL
Mike George
Smashes all the myths about LOVE.
Paperback: 978-1-84694-288-4 ebook: 978-1-84694-682-0

The Holy Spirit's Interpretation of the New Testament
A Course in Understanding and Acceptance
Regina Dawn Akers
Following on from the strength of *A Course In Miracles*, NTI
teaches us how to experience the love and oneness of God.
Paperback: 978-1-84694-085-9 ebook: 978-1-78099-083-5

The Message of A Course In Miracles
A translation of the text in plain language
Elizabeth A. Cronkhite
A translation of *A Course in Miracles* into plain, everyday
language for anyone seeking inner peace. The companion
volume, *Practicing A Course In Miracles*, offers practical lessons
and mentoring.
Paperback: 978-1-84694-319-5 ebook: 978-1-84694-642-4

Rising in Love
My Wild and Crazy Ride to Here and Now, with Amma, the
Hugging Saint
Ram Das Batchelder
Rising in Love conveys an author's extraordinary journey of
spiritual awakening with the Guru, Amma.
Paperback: 978-1-78279-687-9 ebook: 978-1-78279-686-2

Thinker's Guide to God
Peter Vardy
An introduction to key issues in the philosophy of religion.
Paperback: 978-1-90381-622-6

Your Simple Path
Find happiness in every step
Ian Tucker
A guide to helping us reconnect with what is really important in
our lives.
Paperback: 978-1-78279-349-6 ebook: 978-1-78279-348-9

365 Days of Wisdom
Daily Messages To Inspire You Through The Year
Dadi Janki
Daily messages which cool the mind, warm the heart and guide
you along your journey.
Paperback: 978-1-84694-863-3 ebook: 978-1-84694-864-0

Body of Wisdom
Women's Spiritual Power and How it Serves
Hilary Hart
Bringing together the dreams and experiences of women across
the world with today's most visionary spiritual teachers.
Paperback: 978-1-78099-696-7 ebook: 978-1-78099-695-0

Dying to Be Free
From Enforced Secrecy to Near Death to True Transformation
Hannah Robinson
After an unexpected accident and near-death experience, Hannah
Robinson found herself radically transforming her life, while a
remarkable new insight altered her relationship with her father, a
practising Catholic priest.
Paperback: 978-1-78535-254-6 ebook: 978-1-78535-255-3

The Ecology of the Soul
A Manual of Peace, Power and Personal Growth for Real People
in the Real World
Aidan Walker
Balance your own inner Ecology of the Soul to regain your
natural state of peace, power and wellbeing.
Paperback: 978-1-78279-850-7 ebook: 978-1-78279-849-1

Not I, Not other than I
The Life and Teachings of Russel Williams
Steve Taylor, Russel Williams
The miraculous life and inspiring teachings of one of the World's
greatest living Sages.
Paperback: 978-1-78279-729-6 ebook: 978-1-78279-728-9

On the Other Side of Love
A Woman's Unconventional Journey Towards Wisdom
Muriel Maufroy
When life has lost all meaning, what do you do?
Paperback: 978-1-78535-281-2 ebook: 978-1-78535-282-9

Practicing A Course In Miracles
A Translation of the Workbook in Plain Language and With
Mentoring Notes
Elizabeth A. Cronkhite
The practical second and third volumes of The Plain-Language
A Course In Miracles.
Paperback: 978-1-84694-403-1 ebook: 978-1-78099-072-9

Quantum Bliss
The Quantum Mechanics of Happiness, Abundance, and Health
George S. Mentz
Quantum Bliss is the breakthrough summary of success and spirituality secrets that customers have been waiting for.
Paperback: 978-1-78535-203-4 ebook: 978-1-78535-204-1

The Upside Down Mountain
Mags MacKean
A must-read for anyone weary of chasing success and happiness – one woman's inspirational journey swapping the uphill slog for the downhill slope.
Paperback: 978-1-78535-171-6 ebook: 978-1-78535-172-3

Your Personal Tuning Fork
The Endocrine System
Deborah Bates
Discover your body's health secret, the endocrine system, and 'twang' your way to sustainable health!
Paperback: 978-1-84694-503-8 ebook: 978-1-78099-697-4

Readers of ebooks can buy or view any of these bestsellers by clicking on the live link in the title. Most titles are published in paperback and as an ebook. Paperbacks are available in traditional bookshops. Both print and ebook formats are available online.

Find more titles and sign up to our readers' newsletter at
http://www.johnhuntpublishing.com/mind-body-spirit

Follow us on Facebook at https://www.facebook.com/OBooks/
and Twitter at https://twitter.com/obooks